TEN BEST WESTERN FLYFISHING DESTINATIONS

From The INSIDE ANGLER

Michael Fong
Photography by Michael and Christine Fong

Photography by Michael and Christine Fong

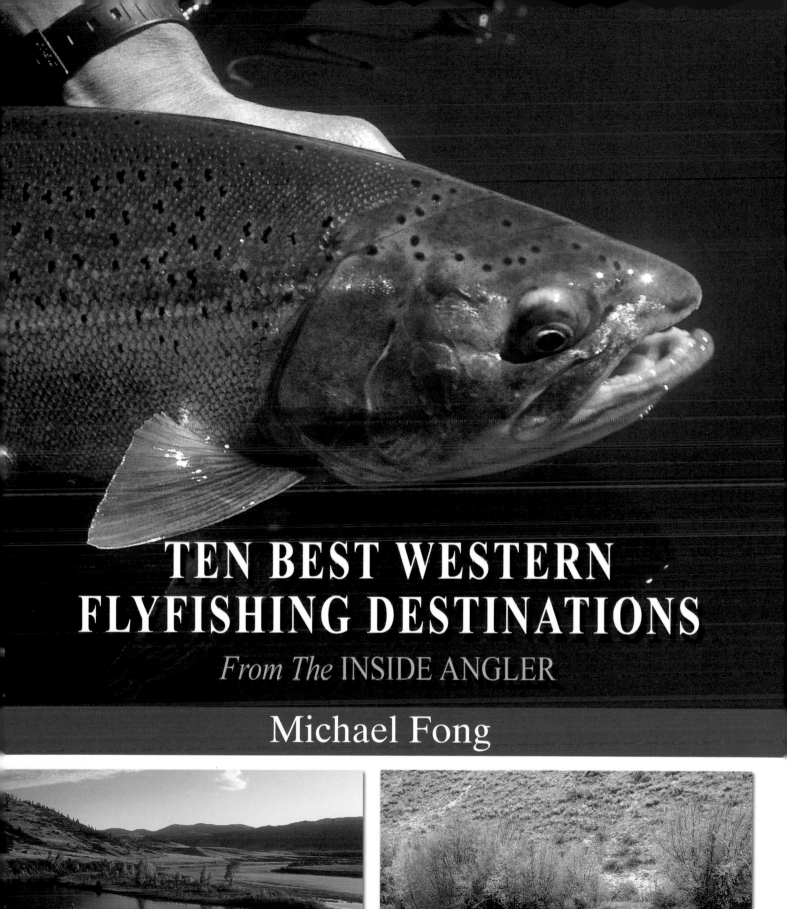

TEN BEST WESTERN FLYFISHING DESTINATIONS

From The INSIDE ANGLER

Michael Fong

Frank
Amato
PORTLAND

Michael Fong, the author.

Acknowledgments

Since we have gained our livelihood in large part from engaging in fishing and fly fishing in particular, we must acknowledge that without those that swim on the earth, we wouldn't have been able to enjoy fishing and in turn share the information gathered with our newsletter subscribers. When I think back over the perhaps 200 destinations published in *The Inside Angler* the number of people to thank would be tremendous and would include our subscribers, guides, outfitters, lodge and shop owners and a multitude of friendly people we met during our travels. With regard to these ten best reports appreciation goes to: Clark Canyon Reservoir, MT, Tim Tollett and Darrelle and Ron Vecchio; Dean River, BC, Judy Hill and in tribute Tony Hill, Daryl Hodson and Ron Tanouye; Eagle Lake, CA, Jay Fair; Elk River BC, Jim Crawford, John Kendal and Kelly Laatsch; Green River, WY, Bennie Johnson; Lower Sacramento River, CA, Mike and Bertha Michalak, Mike Mercer, Brad Jackson, Ernie Denison, Barry Foster, and Jim Murphy; Missouri River, MT, Pete Cardinal, Jim Crawford, and Tim Plaska; Rogue River, OR, Al Perryman, Gary Anderson, Noah, and Gary Warren; South Fork Boise, ID, Clayne Baker; Williamson River, OR, Ed Miranda Sr, Ed Miranda Jr, Rich Henry, Steve and Debbie Hilbert.

Don Bauders, Mike's bass fishing partner, introduced us to Moon Ma of K K Graphics. We acknowledge all at K K Graphics, notably Moon Ma, Phil Ma, Julie Ma and Jack Szeto, for their expertise and excellence in pre-pressing and printing *The Inside Angler* since its inception in January of 1992.

Corin, our daughter has been copy editor for 10 years and has given of her limited free time to support us in our newsletter. In addition, numerous family members, friends and colleagues have given support and valuable advice, namely, Mel and Fanny Krieger, Nelson Ishiyama and Terrie McDonald, Bob Nauheim, Ralph, and Lisa Cutter, Bien and Marie Lee.

Richard Anderson and Dave Inks were the original producers of the Tote 'N Float and Water Master boats which we used for many years in our destinations.

Our long-time sponsors Fenwick (Pure Fishing) and Umpqua Feather Merchants deserve sincere appreciation, also Abel, G. Loomis, Patagonia, Redington, and Scientific Anglers.

I wish to thank Frank Amato, Kim Koch, Ann Amato, Esther Poleo and all at Frank Amato Publications for their patience and support.

Christine Fong, October 2002
San Francisco, CA

Published in 2003 by
FRANK AMATO PUBLICATIONS, INC.
PO Box 82112 • Portland, Oregon 97282 • (503) 653-8108
Softbound ISBN: 1-57188-287-1 • Softbound UPC: 0-81127-00108-8

Photography by Michael Fong and Christine Fong
Book Design: Esther Poleo
Printed in Hong Kong

Contents

*This book is dedicated to the memory of Michael Fong,
devoted husband, father, conservationist and a friend to
fly-fishers everywhere*

Introduction

For most of my life, beginning shortly after I began elementary school, I've been fascinated by fishing. It is a passion to which I've devoted the majority of my time exceeded by only making enough money to support a family and by family obligations. Throughout most of my life, I've placed fishing ahead of just about everything and it shouldn't be surprising that most of my closest friends are anglers. One of the things that made this possible was that my wife, Chris, also fished. This was not the case when we first met as students at the California College of Arts & Crafts in Oakland, California in the late 50s and then married. We moved to Iowa City where I was offered a teaching assistant position in the art department at the University of Iowa and studied for a Masters of Fine Arts degree in painting and drawing. If the truth were known, my classes were by arrangement and I spent much more time fishing than at the University. Chris loved the outdoors and photography became one of her main interests. At first, she photographed nature and then she began to record my fishing exploits. All this was done while she was doing the major share of raising Corin, our daughter. After our return to the Bay Area in California, when Corin was young and didn't accompany us fishing, she spent many weekends with Chris' parents. By this time, Chris began to fish and it wasn't long before she became a flyfisher too. As Corin grew older, she also enjoyed fishing. Because her interests were more varied, she wasn't consumed by the activity nearly as much as Chris and myself.

Working as a writer/ photographer team, Chris and I were able to sell freelance fishing articles to national outdoor periodicals.

For many years, beginning in the late 60s, we sold articles primarily about flyfishing to *Outdoor Life, Field & Stream, and Sports Afield*. To readers of outdoor magazines, these were known as the "Big Three" because they were the highest-circulation periodicals that published stories about fishing and hunting. We also sold articles to the *Garcia Fishing Annual, Fishing World, Saltwater Sportsmen* and others. This was at a time when selling a story brought reasonable financial returns, paying as much as some magazines pay today, thirty years later. In the late 70s, I assumed the editorship of *The Flyfisher*, the magazine of the Federation of Fly Fishers, a position I held for five years. It was around this time that some national outdoor publications began to publish regional sections for specific areas of the country hoping to maintain their large circulations as regional outdoor publications were springing up. A change was taking place in outdoor publishing with special interest publications coming to market too. It was about this time that *Fly Fisherman Magazine* was started. After a time, I became a contributing editor.

During all this time, my fishing could only be described as a hobby. The money needed to support a household came from a regular job in the graphic arts, a career that lasted for twenty-seven years. My employer in San Francisco was Gregory & Falk, a family-owned, union business, which treated its employees with a lot of compassion. For about half the years when I was employed, the company arranged my schedule so I could work four days a week. This allowed for plenty of time to fish when added to three weeks of annual vacation and paid holidays. In my last five years with Gregory & Falk, I worked only three days a week because the business was facing a decided downturn. Electronic publishing was making inroads against the old ways of doing lithography and it was coming on faster than most people in the industry imagined. It was plain to see that what I did to support my family was not going to continue providing the financial security it once did.

In 1991, while having dinner at a Japanese restaurant in San Francisco, Chris, Corin and I started talking about beginning our own fishing publication. We decided to call it *The Inside Angler*. I would do the writing and put the publication together; Chris would be the photographer and circulation manager; and Corin would be our copy editor. Corin had graduated from the University of California at Berkeley and finished her advanced degree from Harvard and was well on her way to establishing her own career. Her involvement would only be part-time so we could use her command of the English language to clean up the copy. *The Inside Angler* would be a newsletter reporting on the most productive fly-fishing destinations in western North America. We would present unbiased, first-hand reports illustrated with high-quality black-and-white photographs and detailed maps showing exactly the location of the fishing. There would be no advertising to influence our editorial opinions, but if we encountered services that made our fishing more enjoyable and more rewarding, we certainly wouldn't hesitate to recommend them. In order for our reports to be as useful as possible, we would list prices for a wide range of services including places to stay and eat. If the preparation of food was better than average and the restaurant or lodge took pride in their kitchen and it showed, we would point this out too. It would be exactly the kind of information we would appreciate if we were traveling to a fishing destination new to us. In January 1992, we began publishing *The Inside Angler*. The very technology that was making my skills as a lithographer less in demand was allowing Chris and myself the chance to be part-time desktop publishers and near full-time anglers. This was ironic.

At the beginning of 1993, when our renewal notices were sent out and began to return, it became clear that what began as a dream was becoming a reality. Not only did our subscribers like the information we provided, many of them recommended our flyfishing newsletter to angling friends. Although I had seniority in my department at Gregory & Falk and could have stayed on, I gave notice for early retirement to pursue a life as a wandering angler traveling with a laptop computer. With a daughter who had become a successful administrator, Chris and I traveled constantly in search for interesting and productive fly-fishing destinations on behalf of our subscribers for whom we worked as professional correspondents. It's a life Chris and I thoroughly enjoyed and we never lost sight of the fact that it is our subscribers who made it possible. If we had a motto

to describe the reporting in our newsletters, it would be along the lines that if we thought the fishing had potential and we enjoyed ourselves, then we would report on it.

Since beginning *The Inside Angler*, we have reported on more than 200 destinations with most of these lakes and streams found in western North America. From these, Chris and I have selected ten waters that we consider to be outstanding. In our opinion, each stream or lake has one or more significant reasons to make it stand apart. In the introduction to each report that was originally filed in *The Inside Angler*, we provide information to bring the report up to date and explain why we believe a visit is worth your time. Chris and I hope that you have the opportunity to visit these lakes and streams and discover for yourselves some of the finest fishing the world has to offer. In order to keep up with the advances in electronic communication, *The Inside Angler* has its web site at www.insideangler.com. If you have any questions regarding flyfishing, with an emphasis on destinations in the West or would like to post a message to share fishing information, please visit our discussion/bulletin board at "Heads & Tails." It will be time well invested.

CLARK CANYON RESERVOIR

CLARK CANYON RESERVOIR

*I*f Chris and I were not continually seeking out new waters to fish, we would certainly spend more time fishing at Clark Canyon Reservoir than we do. Not only has it remained a productive and dependable fishery through the years, the methods that are successful for catching fish are fun to employ. The rainbows and browns average two to three pounds and grow quickly to five. Some approach double digits in weight. However, size and numbers are not the only things that we use to judge a fishery. What we like about fishing at Clark Canyon are the fish themselves. The rainbows grow thick through the middle and act as if they're bonefish when they rush off after being hooked. When the hook is set, it's as if a race starter just fired off their pistol. If you happen to be raising the rod at the same moment a rainbow grabs your fly and leaves the scene, say good-bye to your fly and 3x tippet. For those anglers who say that a reel is only used to hold the fly line and never comes into play while trying to land a trout, be prepared for a new experience. Where the rainbows of Clark Canyon possess the profile of a middle-distance runner, the browns are like street fighters. They know no rules of combat and most often head straight for the bottom to foul the leader. It becomes a tug-of-war, testing within ounces the strength of your chosen tippet size. Nearly all the trout that Chris and I have caught in Clark Canyon act and look like they were born in the wild as opposed to a hatchery. The reason for this is that many were planted in the lake when they were only four to six inches long and the fertility of the water allows them to grow strong rapidly. There is also some natural reproduction in the Red Rock River flowing from the south and the streams entering from the west.

The Lone Tree Campground has level areas next to the shoreline to set up camp. This makes it convenient for anglers to tie up their boats close to their RVs and trailers. Mosquitoes can be a problem for those setting camp close to the water. To avoid the biting bugs, some anglers choose to set camp on high ground a good distance away from the shoreline.

Mike removes a Sheep Creek Special from a rainbow before it is released.

The typical Clark Canyon rainbow weighs between two and three pounds. It would not be unusual to hook fish much larger during a productive session.

There are some anglers who do little more than drag a Woolly Bugger behind a float tube and consider that this might be the essence of fishing stillwater. You can catch trout at Clark Canyon Reservoir by trolling, but it wouldn't be the most productive way to present a fly, or the most satisfying. In fishing stillwater, I believe most anglers who take pride in their skills continually look forward to the challenge of trying to uncover a strategy that best mimics the food forms that trout are keying on at the moment. It can change more than once through the course of a day. The foods that are available to trout are influenced by the season, but just as importantly, the proximity of the food to where trout find the most comfort is part of the riddle that needs to be solved before success is met regularly. The Inside Angler has filed two reports on Clark Canyon Reservoir. In Volume I, Number 2, March 15, 1992, we looked at the fishing after summer had set in and trout retreated to deeper water for most of the day. For fishing earlier in the season when many trout come into the shallows to feed, an update report was filed in Volume IV, Number 6, November 15, 1995. To be chronologically consistent with the season, we combined the two reports presenting the update report first, followed by the one we did in our first year of publishing. Chris and I have fished at Clark

Canyon numerous times through the years, the latest visit taking place in 1999.

As mentioned in the reports, camping is free at Clark Canyon, unless you choose to stay at the private facility near the dam that has hookups for RVs. For the price of a state fishing license, it's free to fish. In a time when private, managed fisheries are springing up like politicians on the heels of undecided voters, Clark Canyon can provide quality fishing with the added satisfaction that any fish caught is well earned.

CLARK CANYON RESERVOIR

Clark Canyon Reservoir in Montana is located twenty miles south of Dillon on Interstate 15 at an elevation of 5,500 feet. At the bottom of Clark Canyon Reservoir was a place called Camp Fortunate. It was here that the Lewis and Clark Expedition left provisions for their safe return down the Missouri after their exploration of the Northwest. A chance meeting between Sacajawea, their native guide for the expedition, and Cameawaite, her brother, was indeed fortunate. This is the reason many landmarks in the area, such as campgrounds, bear Native American names. In the inundation of Camp Fortunate about 160 years after the expedition, an excellent stillwater fishery was born.

The flyfishing on the lake has been outstanding for larger-than-average trout almost every year since our first visit in 1991. One of our visits took place in mid June 1994. It came on the heels of some of the heaviest winter snowfall and spring and early summer precipitation on record. In our travels to locate better-than-average fishing, we went to Clark Canyon Reservoir after finding that most of the streams flowing off the west slope of the Continental Divide were high with turbid flows. The prevailing weather was swinging wildly from warm, pleasant days to outbursts of thunderstorms, hail, wind and heavy rain. The Red Rock River flowing into Clark Canyon was high and discolored, and the lake level was the highest since 1984 and still rising. All the shoreline shelters available for use by campers at the south side of the lake were partially submerged. Only the roofs of some were visible. These made popular resting places for flocks of gulls. During this time, anglers at Clark Canyon Reservoir were enjoying some of the best still water fishing in the West.

On our arrival, we heard that the fishing was productive near Hap Hawkins campground on the southwest side of the lake. Taking the dirt road from the south that leads to Lone Tree Campground, we headed west past Lone Tree where there were as many as 25 parties camping or staying in recreational vehicles. One and one half miles past Lone Tree, we came to the road that leads to Hap Hawkins. Along the way we saw a band of antelope, a common sight at Clark Canyon. Hap Hawkins can be reserved by groups, but can also be used by individuals. The only developments are outhouses and a large, roofed shelter with a wood-burning grill. Like all the campgrounds around the lake, there are no shade trees. There was only one other party at Hap Hawkins. This couple was set up in their travel trailer. We parked our van conversion near the shelter on one of the few level spots and prepared dinner. That evening it was clear and breezy and we did not fish.

At 6:30 the next morning, I looked out a window to find the water calm. There were very few rises and as Chris rested, I launched my Watermaster inflatable. With a floating line, I began to cover the water fishing a #14 Flashback Nymph on a six-inch dropper 36 inches above a #6 Sheep Creek. The dropper was 4x as was the tippet. The technique I employed was to cast the two flies out to a distance of about 60 to 70 feet and let them fall slowly. If I didn't get a strike after counting to 30, I would begin a slow retrieve. Using this method, I fished from a bay to the east to a steep outcrop to the west, a distance of 200 yards. Because it was shallow along the bank, I stayed from 100 to 150 feet from the shoreline. Every now and then, a fish rose, but never within casting range. For two hours, I never had a strike.

Before returning to the van for breakfast, I decided to try something different. With another outfit rigged with a Type II shooting taper and a #8 Black Marabou Leech, I began to troll. About 100 feet out from camp, I hooked and landed a 17-inch rainbow. Shortly afterward, I had another strike, but this turned out to be a sucker about the same size as the rainbow. It was definitely time for breakfast.

Through breakfast, I kept an eye on the water and saw no rises. A light breeze began to blow and Callibaetis spinners took to the air. From other experiences on Clark Canyon, midmorning was a good time to fish, but fish movement at Hap Hawkins was nil. I did not expect to see lots of rising fish, but enough surface activity to let me know that fish were present and active. Clark Canyon is not known as a lake that provides consistent dry-fly fishing.

As soon as we could pack our things and load up the van, we headed back toward Lone Tree.

On the way, the road rises to a high spot, which allows the viewing of a large part of the lake. Off in the distance, we could see the single tree that marked the campground and the boat launch nearby. On the side of the ramp nearest to us was a point leading out into the lake lined with submerged willows. Nearer still was a bay that backed up nearly to the road. A car was parked near the South Bay Access, which is nothing more than a dirt road leading to the water. Directly out toward the lake from us along the shoreline was a 4-wheel-drive vehicle. Three anglers in float tubes were fishing near the SUV. With binoculars, we could see fish moving near these three anglers, but no fish were hooked in the fifteen minutes that we watched. This was the only area where fish movement was observed. We then headed for Lone Tree.

It was now about 12:30. On either side of the unpaved boat launch, the shoreline slopes gently to the water making the launching of personal flotation crafts easy. If you wanted to camp or park your RV near the water, this was also easy. Those with boats could beach their equipment close to their rigs. Because mosquitoes were more numerous along the shoreline, some anglers chose to camp away from the water on higher ground. There were many places with level terrain. If you decide to overnight at Lone Tree, a consideration of where to camp might be influenced by where you want to fish. Red Rock River enters the lake to the east. Although it is too far to go to the river mouth in a personal flotation device, you will find deep water close to the bank by heading in that direction. When fish feed, they often move from deep water into the shallows. The sloping transition zones from deep to shallow water are always productive places to fish. I saw quite a few anglers with sonar units capable of detecting water depth. The newest units also have the ability to scan horizontally. These electronic devices can help you find the transition zones and even detect swimming fish. Without one of these units, you can still find the drop-offs at Clark Canyon by sight because the water is clear. Once I find one of these places, I like to position myself on the shallows and make my presentations out to deeper water. In this way, I

Chris shows the brown taken on a small imitation of a Callibaetis may fly before it is released.

Chris is about to land a brown hooked on a dry fly. The fish was seen rising in the lee of a line of willows advancing into the water.

have the fish coming to me instead of making presentations to trout that have already overrun my position.

Although there were still many anglers fishing, some were concluding their morning's efforts. Every now and then a trout was hooked, but the peak of the fishing had passed. I spoke to several anglers and the consensus seemed to be that nearly everyone hooked at least one trout, but some had caught and released a dozen or more. The majority of the trout were rainbows with some big browns also taken. The size of the trout ranged from 18 to 28 inches. All were hooked with either nymphs or leech-type flies. For fishing nymphs, floating lines were employed. Anglers either fished two nymphs in combination or singles by letting the flies slowly sink or used indicators ten feet above the suspended flies. Sink-tip and full-sinking lines were used to fish swimming flies like damselfly nymphs, leeches and buggers at greater depths. These were presented either by trolling or by casting and retrieving. Because trout often struck the flies hard, 3x tippets were the choice of most anglers. Even so, break-offs were common. When a trout took your fly, it was best to set the hook by making a long draw with the line hand. If connection to a fish was made, you had to be ready to release your hold on the line immediately. Raising the rod quickly while holding tight to the line was not a good thing to do. During a session a few days later, I was fishing a nymph beneath an indicator when it disappeared when I wasn't looking. Instead of drawing the line tight, I began to raise the rod. I hadn't even gotten it to 45 degrees when the tip suddenly jerked to the water. It seemed that eight-pound-test tippet would stand more abuse than that, but it didn't. The rainbows at Clark Canyon are known for their quick, sustained, high-speed runs after taking the fly. This is another reason why fishing at Clark Canyon is so much fun. It tests the tackle as well as the angler.

Although the fishing had slowed, Chris and I were anxious to hook a fish. We found a place to park our van conversion to the east of the launch ramp. An angler in a boat called out to us as soon as we got onto the water. It was Fred Penfield from Reno. He had attended one of our clinics given through the Reno Fly Shop. Fred said the fishing had

been great that morning and among the many trout he landed was a 6 1/2-pound brown. Through the rest of the afternoon, Fred hooked several more trout and Chris and I had only two between us. The wind came up a bit, but not so strongly that it inhibited our movement. In the breeze it was difficult to hold our exact positions without drifting ever so slightly. To the unknowing, this movement is akin to drag when fishing a stream. It can mean the difference between catching a few trout as opposed to many. Knowing how to deal with this unwanted movement and the resulting action it negatively imparts to the fly is sometimes critical when fishing at Clark Canyon. Staying stationary is the only way you can have complete control when making presentations.

Anglers catch fish by trolling or retrieving a fly at Clark Canyon, but on most occasions, trout will respond most favorably to a fly that is slowly settling. The best way to control your fly is fishing from a stationary position. From a boat, this means anchoring fore and aft. When the wind frequently changes directions, this is the only way to remain stationary. You can usually get by with one anchor when fishing from a float tube or other personal flotation devices. However, most anglers fishing from personal inflatables rarely carry an anchor. This can be a big mistake. A 3-pound salmon trolling weight can serve as an anchor. A netted bag filled with rocks is a popular anchor as is a plastic container with a molded handle filled with sand. You can also purchase a folding anchor made specifically for lightweight boats and canoes.

If you find yourself without an anchor when you need one, you can maintain your position by using your cast line as a marker. Choose a place where fish have shown on the surface or where there is structure, like a drop-off. Cast the fly or flies so they land with the line as straight as possible. If the line isn't straight, retrieve some of the line to make it so. Once this is done, maneuver only when necessary. Since you can only move backwards when kicking with your fins, it's important that you cast downwind to the area that you want to fish. This will require that you either kick straight back or to either side to maintain your position. Also, feeding fish are usually heading into the wind and you will often have targets to cast to.

Chris and I didn't have anchors that afternoon and I attribute our lack of success partly due to this oversight. The winds were irregular, blowing first from one direction and then from another. I can't say we would have caught more fish if we had anchors, but we could have fished more con-

If you stand on the bluff overlooking the north shoreline, it is possible to see by the change in the color of the water where the shallows end and deep water begins. It is a good strategy to make your presentations from the drop-off to deep water.

fidently and it would not have been necessary to keep kicking our fins constantly, which became laborious.

After that first day, we fished at Clark Canyon for six more days. During one of those days, we shot a segment for the "Charles West's Outdoor Gazette" TV show. On that day, it was very windy. Tim Tollett of Frontier Anglers in Dillon helped us with the shoot and I thought we would have to work hard to catch some fish on camera. As it turned out, we caught rainbows throughout the day. The area that we fished was out from the line of submerged willows to the west of the boat launch. We chose this area because it was away from the majority of anglers and a friend of Tim's reported that he had caught fish there the day before.

We had intended to do the standup opening for the TV segment at the overlook by the dam, but the wind was blowing so hard in the morning that the sound quality was poor. For all of our stay, when the wind blew, it came from the south or southwest quadrant. This made fishing from the south shoreline the best choice. Another reason for choosing this area to fish was that it had the most extensive shallows. Shallow parts of lakes warm more quickly than deeper areas, promoting earlier hatches. When hatches occur and wind becomes a factor, you want the wind to blow from the shallows to deeper water. This kind of food flow encourages trout resting in the depths to come inshore to feed. At Clark Canyon this phenomena is readily apparent during Callibaetis hatches combined with winds that come from the south.

Although we had days without wind, strong winds in the afternoon were always a possibility. These winds could come up so suddenly that if you were caught in a float tube 100 yards from shore, it would be nearly impossible to kick back. One morning around 10:00, I started fishing off the submerged willows to the west of the boat launch. A light breeze was blowing and I could see rainbows on the surface every once in a while advancing toward my position. Using the two-fly cast with a Flashback Nymph and Sheep Creek, I landed three rainbows weighing 2 1/2 to 3 1/2 pounds before Chris came out to join me. The breeze was steady and shifting direction, but there was always a lee behind the willows and this is where we fished.

The emergence of Callibaetis became stronger and more fish began to show. As is normally the case when there is a breeze, the rainbows were moving rapidly covering a lot of water to feed. What I try to do is spot cruising fish and

then cast my two nymphs 20 to 30 feet in front of them. If my cast is in line with the cruising trout, the fish will usually find my flies. I only move my flies enough to keep in contact with them if the wind creates slack.

Shortly after beginning to fish, Chris hooked a nice fish but it got off. A bit later, I landed a rainbow of 20 inches. I was fishing off the end of the willows out in the open and Chris had positioned herself in the lee. She called over to say that a number of fish were taking emerging duns and that she was going to try a #16 Adams Paradun. Moments later, she let out a scream and I looked over to see a good bend in her rod. Instead of taking off and making a long run like a rainbow, this fish put up a deepwater fight trying to dislodge the fly by catching the leader on the bottom debris. Each time the fish was brought near the surface, it would dive back down to the bottom. Five minutes passed before Chris was able to net the brown. It measured more than 23 inches.

When we resumed fishing, the wind gained in intensity. A chop came on the water, but rainbows could still be seen rolling into the waves. I had just moved back to the end of the willows when a strong gust of wind made me kick harder to maintain my position. A second gust made me kick even harder and I headed back to the lee to join Chris. Within a couple of minutes, the wind began to howl and the surface of the lake was churning. We oared our crafts into little coves surrounded by willows and hung on. For fifteen minutes the wind was unrelenting. The velocity must have been 30 to 40 miles per hour. If it weren't for hanging onto the willows, we would have been blown out to open water. These heavy winds continued on and off through the afternoon and although we each landed another rainbow, it cut short our fishing day.

There is a launch ramp for trailered boats at the Lone Tree Campground on the south side of the lake. During years of heavy winter precipitation, when the lake level is very high the following spring, the angle of the launching area may be very gradual requiring that the trailer be backed a good distance into the lake before the boat is floating.

When the lake level is low, it is possible to drive down to the lake's edge to launch inflatables or portable boats. Take care not to drive too close to the water as the ground may be too soft for good traction.

Chris brings a brown toward her float tube.

The shoreline off South Beach can be a productive place to fish in the early season. Seen to the east is the Lone Tree Campground, marked by the single tree at the point. The bay to the right of South Beach can also be a good place to fish in the early season.

On the evenings that we camped at the lake instead of staying in town in a motel or RV park, we sometimes fished by wading the flats to the east of the boat launch. We caught fish using nymphs, but also had the opportunity to cast dry flies to trout that cruised the shoreline. At times, some of these fish were in less than two feet of water. Small trout usually feed in these extreme shallows, but by observing closely, we saw that many of these trout were sizable. The big fish moved steadily along the shoreline and we had to be ready to make presentations quickly or they were soon out of range.

In search of other productive areas, one morning we went to the spot where Chris and I watched anglers fishing after we left Hap Hawkins. When we first saw this place, a dirt road ran along the shoreline so a vehicle could easily be driven right to the spot. The rising waters of the lake had covered this road so we had to launch our inflatables at the South Bay Access. We fished our way to the west and didn't see any fish movement until we were nearly 200 yards from the access. The morning was calm and we fished with Jim Crawford, a long-time friend who recently moved to Polson, Montana after residing for years in British Columbia.

From 10:30 to 2:30, when the wind came up abruptly and blew us off the water, we had constant action for rainbows that weighed from 2 1/2 to five pounds. We also caught a 3 1/2-pound brown. All the fish were caught using the two-nymph combination with half of the fish taking the Flashback Nymph while the others took the Sheep Creek. To the west of us, the shoreline made a sweeping curve out to a point. Off the point was a large island. Another party had come by motorboat and disembarked to fish from float tubes. They also hooked fish.

What I think is important is that we observed no fish activity at the South Bay Access until we were at least 200 yards to the west. The point, that I referred to earlier, separates South Bay from the water near Hap Hawkins. If you want to explore the water where we saw anglers fishing after arriving by boat, there is a dirt road leading to this spot off the road that leads to Hap Hawkins. A barbwire fence keeps cattle from the water, but a gate allows passage for vehicles. Be sure to close the gate behind you if you fish here.

If you would like to fish by wading, you might consider fishing where the Red Rock River enters the lake. The rough road from the south was the original road to Dillon and if you don't turn west toward Lone Tree, it will lead right into the lake. If you want to launch a small boat or a personal flotation device here, it is very easy. There are no shoulders on the two-lane road and it could be very difficult to turn a large RV around. The day we drove to the end of the road, we saw bait anglers catching good-sized rainbows. It was late in the afternoon and we saw a few fish break the surface out of range of their bobbers suspending night crawlers. If we weren't on our way to town, we would have launched our inflatables to fish.

To fish the entering stream, park your vehicle at the pull-out by the cattle guard in line with the fence. If you walk towards the willows, you will find the Red Rock River as it enters the lake. The course of the river winds and turns and fish hide beneath undercuts at the bends. Marty and Mike Heard, owners of the Buffalo Lodge Steakhouse and Saloon just east of the dam, told us we should fish Woolly Buggers and leech patterns on sink-tip lines. They and other flyfishers had caught rainbows larger than 25 inches near the time of our visit. We drove past this parking area for the stream many times during our visit and only on one occasion did we see a vehicle.

As the heat of summer warms the shallows, the best daytime fishing is no longer found on the south side of Clark Canyon Reservoir. In the morning and evening, trout still come onto the flats, but the sessions are short. During July and August, we concentrate our fishing off the deeper north side. Hatches of Callibaetis are still present, but the movement of feeding trout is different than earlier in the season and our tactics differ too. First we look for signs of fish on the surface. These summer fish are gregarious and if you see a fish or two coming to the surface in an area, it normally means there are more fish below. Unlike fishing on the flats in the spring, you normally don't see a lot of fish on the surface. After quietly moving to within casting range, we make

a long cast into the area. Our tackle is set up exactly like we do when fishing in the spring. At the point, we used a #6 Sheep Creek. This fly is notable for its simplicity and is tied with two winds of brown hackle at where the bend of the hook begins. The body is wrapped with variegated chenille and a few wisps of mallard breast feathers tied on top like a wet fly. It is a fine fish catcher at times, but is mainly used in this instance for another purpose.

Three feet up from the Sheep Creek, on a six-inch dropper of 4x (6-pound test), is tied a #14 or #16 Flashback Nymph or a Pheasant Tail Nymph in the same size. When using this two-fly combination for the Callibaetis hatch, it would not be unusual to hook fish only on the smaller flies and none on the Sheep Creek. The Sheep Creek, because of its good sink rate, is used to assist the lighter Flashback to significant depths. Cast out as straight a line as you can and let the flies sink very slowly without imparting any action. Fish the flies until you think they have reached a depth of ten to 15 feet or about a slow 40 count. If a fish hasn't taken the offering, retrieve the flies in a slow, steady draw so they move toward the surface and let the flies fall again.

To fish this method properly, the leader must float except where it breaks the surface. If you find the whole leader sinking, strikes will be difficult to see. When this happens, clean the leader with a dry cloth and use fly floatant or Musclin to prepare the leader.

Most of your strikes will come when the flies are slowly falling. When a trout takes your fly, it's seen as a subtle increase in the sink rate, a lateral movement where the leader breaks the surface or if the leader signals the flies are no longer sinking. Each of these signs could only mean that the flies have been intercepted. The latter occurs when a fish takes the fly and holds it in its mouth deciding whether it's something good to eat.

When fishing Clark Canyon in summer, we often camp at a site on the north side and take a short drive or walk with our float boats down to the lake. By standing on an overlook, you can see where the shallows end and the deep water begins. There is a definite color change. Except in the early morning when some fish cruise the shallows and are fun to chase, we mostly fish in deeper water close to the drop-offs looking for signs of activity. The deep water is sometimes close to shore. If the lake level is low, you will see exposed trees following the old creek bed near the middle of the lake. Fish also like to congregate here. When moving from one spot to another in our belly boats, we let our flies trail in the water (trolling). More than once, we've had vicious strikes that have parted our leaders.

Fishing Clark Canyon is a change of pace while visiting the streams in this area. The Beaverhead River flowing from Clark Canyon Reservoir produces some of the largest stream trout in Montana. Poindexter Slough is just minutes south of Dillon if you want to challenge spring-creek trout. If you choose to fish Clark Canyon Reservoir, pick a calm day with as little wind as possible. The most successful method described above only works when winds are light. If you must fish when the wind is blowing, use an indicator placed ten feet up on the leader above the fly.

On the bluff overlooking the lake on the north side are several campgrounds with structures that offer shade and protection from wind. With the exception of the private campground by the dam, there is no charge to camp at Clark Canyon Reservoir. It is a good idea to bring your own drinking water, especially if the water table is low.

SUMMARY

Clark Canyon Reservoir provides good fishing, particularly in the early season when fish are found in the shallows. For those who like to camp or have an RV, it's possible to find a site by the water and have fish feeding at your doorstep. This is a very attractive situation and many stillwater enthusiasts take advantage of this opportunity.

In addition to the area around Lone Tree and the South Bay Access, another place you might try fishing is where Horse Prairie Creek enters on the southwest corner. Every time we passed this place, we saw at least one parked vehicle. A dirt road leads down to the shore very near where the creek enters. According to Jim and Shirley McAndrews at the Southside RV Park in Dillon, where we sometimes spend the night, this is a very productive area to fish in the early season. Jim is a long-time resident of the area who is an avid angler. We found him very willing to suggest places to fish that anglers from out of the area might be unfamiliar. If you have a RV and seek a place to set up in Dillon, Jim's fishing information alone makes his RV Park far superior to the KOA Campground run by non-fishing folks.

It's impossible to forecast the exact fishing conditions one will encounter from season to season. It would be unusual for the waters of Clark Canyon to be as high in late spring as they were in 1995. No matter what the conditions might be, I believe you will still find good fishing on the south side of the lake before summer temperatures drive the fish from the shallows. In a visit in 1999, a big school of fish had gathered to the east of where the Red Rock River emptied into the lake. For up-to-date fishing information, call a local fly shop.

Businesses

The following are some of the businesses near Clark Canyon and in Dillon. For a more complete listing, contact the DILLON CHAMBER OF COMMERCE, 125 South Montana Street, Dillon, MT 59725; Tel. 406-683-5511. Camping is free on the reservoir at the public campgrounds, but bring your own drinking water as a precaution. During drought years, the water at the campgrounds may not be safe to drink.

Motels

• BEST WESTERN PARADISE INN MOTEL, 660 North Montana Street, Dillon, MT 59725; Tel. 406-683-4214, has rates ranging from $46 to $70. A restaurant and a lounge are located on the premises.

• CENTENNIAL INN, 122 South Washington Street, Dillon, MT 59725; Tel. 406-683-4454, has four rooms decorated in Victorian themes starting at around $80 offered on a B&B basis. All rooms have private baths. One of the nicest restaurants in Dillon is located on the first floor. Guests can arrange for an early breakfast to suit their fishing schedule.

• CRESTON MOTEL, 335 South Atlantic Street, Dillon, MT 59725; Tel. 406-683-2341, has rooms at moderate prices and is very popular with traveling anglers. The motel is located in a quiet part of town away from the main traffic through the city.

• SUPER 8, 550 North Montana Street, Dillon, MT 59725; Tel. 406-683-4288, has rooms typical of most motels in the chain. Rooms begin at $50.

• GUEST HOUSE, Tel. 406-683-3636

Places to Eat

• THE CENTENNIAL INN (listed with "motels"), serves excellent meals in a Victorian setting. It's one of the finer restaurants in town. Full dinners served with a house salad start at around $15. Wines by the bottle are available.

• PAPA TS, 10 North Montana Street, Dillon, MT 59725; Tel. 406-683-6432, is famous for serving ribs on Wednesday evenings. They sell out fast and if you arrive late, you may have to eat chicken, pizza or have a burger. This is a popular place for families, and prices are moderate.

• PIZZA HUT, 800 North Idaho Street, Dillon, MT 59725; Tel. 406-683-6111, may be the only place to eat for those anglers who stay out late to fish the evening rise.

• WESTERN WOK, 17 East Bannock Street, Dillon, MT 59724; Tel. 406-683-2356, serves Chinese food. We did not find the food anything close to being authentic, but the locals seem to enjoy eating here.

• BUFFALO LODGE, Marty and Mike Heard, Proprietors, 19975 Highway 91 South, Dillon, MT 59725; Tel. 406-683-5535, is the nearest eating establishment to Clark Canyon Reservoir. It is located on the east side of the highway near the dam. Steaks are their specialty. Marty and Mike are avid anglers and provide good fishing information. Many of the guides who float the Beaverhead hang out at the Buffalo Lodge.

• BLACKTAIL STATION, 26 S. Montana Street; Tel. 406-683-6611, serves steaks, seafood, prime rib & Italian, $15 and up for dinner.

Fly Shops

• FRONTIER ANGLERS, Tim Tollett, Proprietor, 680 North Montana Street, Dillon, MT 59725; Tel. 406-683-5276, is a full-service fly shop with rental equipment and guides for Clark Canyon Reservoir. The guide rate for the lake was $350/day for two anglers, which included lunch and flies. Frontier Anglers serves as an agent for many private water fisheries in the area. For those who might want to fish a small spring creek with large browns, rainbows and brookies, inquire about McCoy Spring Creek; 1-800-228-5263; website: www.frontieranglers.com, e-mail: frontieranglers@mcn.net

• BACKCOUNTRY ANGLER, Tom Smith, owner 426 South Atlantic Street, Dillon, MT 59725; Tel. 406-683-3462.

RV Parks

• SOUTHSIDE RV PARK, 104 East Poindexter, Dillon, MT 59725; Tel. 406-683-2244, is located at the south end of town. The owners are hospitable and provide good flyfishing information. Rates are about $17/night for water and electric and $3 more for sewage and TV. Some sites have shade trees.

• THE RED ROCK RV PARK & GOLF COURSE, 505 Sunset West Road, Dillon, MT 59725; Tel. 406-276-3555, is located just south of Clark Canyon Reservoir (see map). The cost is about $15/night with units containing air conditioners and electric heaters for an added charge of $1. On the grounds is a 9-hole, par 3 golf course. The charge for two golfers staying in a RV is an additional $10. There are no shade trees at this RV Park and during our visit to check out the grounds, the mosquitoes were fierce.

• THE BEAVERHEAD MARINA AND RV PARK Tel. 406-683-5556, is located on Clark Canyon Reservoir by the dam. It closes after Thanksgiving and opens in mid March. Hookups for RVs and camping cost about $15/night. Gas is available, but there are no boats for rent. A store is part of the marina.

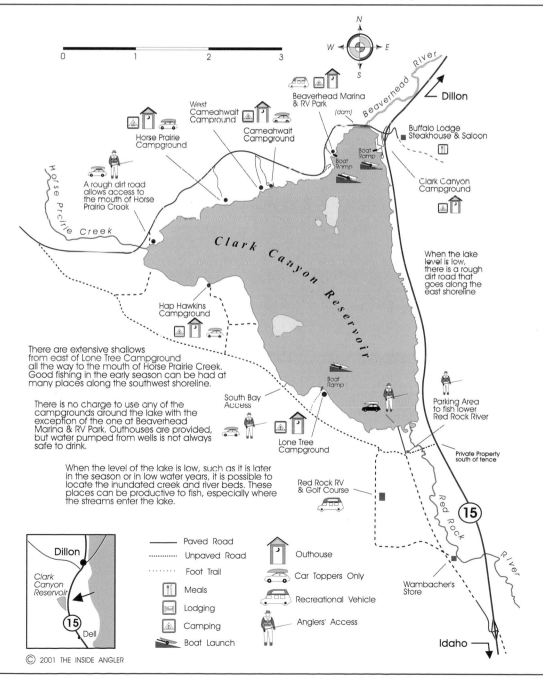

DEAN RIVER

2 West Central
British Columbia Canada

DEAN RIVER

*T*here are steelhead rivers so perfect in their make-up that they stand at the top of the list of locations where devoted steelhead anglers must visit. For summer-run fish, the very best is the Dean River in British Columbia. The Inside Angler reported on the Dean River during our first year of publishing in May 1992. If anything, the fishing has been more consistent or improved since our report.

At the start of our newsletter, Chris and I had an associate who was unknown to our readers. I met Dr. Ron Tanouye several years earlier while on a trip to Norway to fish for Atlantic salmon. This trip was made possible for me through the courtesy of Bob Nauhicm of Fishing International, a long-time friend who was owed a favor by the people who leased a large stretch of the Gaula River. Ron was my fishing partner for the week. He had several successful visits to the Gaula prior to this one. One of the first things we did upon arriving in Trondheim was to go to the local beverage shop to buy some wines and liquors to take with us to the lodge where we would be staying for the week. One of Ron's purchases was a fine bottle of champagne. This was reserved for opening after Ron landed his first salmon of the trip. Each day he placed the champagne in his backpack with some ice in preparation for the anticipated moment.

The cultural experience and camaraderie for the week were memorable, but the fishing was slow. I managed to catch my first Atlantic salmon, followed by three more. Bob landed several including a beauty near 30 pounds, but all Ron caught were grilse, salmon not large enough to be considered adults. On the last evening before our departure, Ron invited Bob and me to his room to enjoy the bottle of champagne. There were no tears shed as we all agreed it was one of the most enjoyable weeks of fishing we had ever had, culminating in making new friendships.

From the river valley floor, mountains rise high on both sides of the river. If you look closely with binoculars, it is possible to see mountain goats on the highest peaks.

For a number of years thereafter, Chris and I traveled to many places to fish with Dr. Tanouye and Kathy, his wife. We had a great trip to Chile where we had access to perhaps the first float plane in the country used to take anglers to remote regions of Patagonia. We chased the elusive steelhead in the panhandle of Alaska from a mother ship towing two jet sleds, fishing some rivers without a name. Ron was top rod on that trip by a mile, demonstrating his skills as an avid steelhead angler. There were many other trips and most of them were in pursuit of steelhead.

Ron's love for wild steelhead was so addictive that the Tanouyes moved from Chicago to Seattle to be closer to the fabled steelhead streams of British Columbia. On an annual basis, Ron fished the Dean from one of the upper river camps and the main stem and the tributaries of the Skeena. As a trauma doctor, he had the means and desire to fish streams that Chris and I could only visit on special occasions. When we began publishing The Inside Angler, Ron was our phantom correspondent. He reported on services that Chris and I couldn't afford to experience except on very special occasions. It was a beautiful match in that we could secure information from a reliable source and combine it with information we gathered to provide a type of reporting that was unique. This was particularly the case on the Dean River.

In September of 1996, Dr. Ron Tanouye drowned while fishing on the Dean River. The Inside Angler lost a valuable component. He will always be remembered in our hearts as a compassionate human being striving to enjoy the journey of life with a fly rod in hand appreciating good food and interesting wines along the way.

Stories of steelhead fishing abound—and some are even true. Once I heard of a couple that fished from one of the upper river camps for many years. The relationship became strained and a divorce took place. In the settlement, the wife took the two rods on the Dean as she was a skilled and

avid angler. I've retold this story a number of times while speaking to angling groups as it's a kind of lament that only a true steelhead angler could appreciate. It also demonstrates how valuable a reserved rod at one of the upper river camps can be. Once an angler gains a spot at one of the two camps above the gorge, it is not relinquished easily. This story does not end here. A few years ago, Chris and I were visiting a fishing lodge in Northern California. The evening meal was served family style allowing guests to enjoy each other's company. As you would expect, fishing was the main topic of conversation. Long into the night with some single malt scotches and vintage wines, a gentleman began to recount on how he used to fish the Dean each year. His current wife listened attentively as he told of how his former wife not only took the two rods they shared on the Dean, but she also ended up with a ranch on Point Reyes on Tomales Bay in California.

Since our report on the Dean, the steelhead fishing has remained about as good as you can expect. Steelhead fishing in any season is a gamble when it comes to river conditions. If you arrive when water flows are constant or dropping, you'll find optimum fishing provided you have the ability to present a fly with a reasonable amount of skill. If it rains, which it can do at any time, and it is heavy, rivers can rise and become discolored making for poor results. Discolored water can also occur when summer temperatures soar. The Sakumtha River and Bernhardt Creek are fed by glaciers and can deposit a lot of sediment into the Dean when hot weather persists. Although the odds of finding less-than-optimum conditions are low to low/moderate, I want to point this out because nothing is guaranteed, especially high returns of steelhead combined with perfect water conditions for any specified week.

You may also want to know that Pittman's operation on the lower river was sold a number of years ago and is now owned by Moose Lake Lodge. Anglers staying here now have the luxury of staying in wood cabins with indoor plumbing. On a visit in 1996, Chris and I enjoyed wonderful meals by as able a camp chef as we've ever encountered. She seemed to cook all day and wore a wind-up clock on a tether around her neck to alert her when items had finished cooking. Another thing I should mention is that those anglers who want to fish the upper river and don't want to go through the chance of the draw and then camp can stay at Nakia Lodge. This lower river lodge has the right to transfer anglers to the stream above the gorge. Moose Lake Lodge, the other lower river camp, does not have a permit

It is best not to beach a steelhead if the shoreline is studded with rocks. The steelhead may injure itself by banging its head on a rock. This beach is sandy and no danger to the steelhead.

for this service. In 1999, Stewart's Lodge on the upper river changed hands and is now under new ownership.

Chris and I hope the information provided here and in our original report lays straight the prospects on fishing the Dean River. We are frequently asked which stream or lake we would choose to fish if limited to one day of fishing. My choice for wild, summer-run steelhead would be the Dean around the first of August, without a moment's hesitation. It's here that all the wonderful things a steelhead angler can imagine have the best chances of coming true. Although fishing from a lodge can be more costly than some anglers wish to spend, the river is not excluded from those of more modest means. Anglers who wish to camp can enter into an annual draw. If chosen, they must make their own arrangements to transport their gear to and from the river. A helicopter from Bella Coola is the manner most popular.

DEAN RIVER

Knowledgeable anglers single out the Dean River in British Columbia as the premier watershed that hosts magnificent summer-run steelhead. Throughout the Pacific range of these sea-going rainbows, relatively few streams sustain runs of native, summer-run fish not yet diluted with hatchery cousins. Though the Dean lies in a remote area, it has not been left untouched. Extensive logging once took place on the watershed, and salmon netting in the Dean Channel took a heavy toll on incidentally caught steelhead with estimates as high as 10,000 fish in some years. During years when salmon returns were great, steelhead fishing was not as good compared to years of fewer salmon. Large returns of salmon allowed for an extended, commercial salmon season and this adversely affected steelhead stocks. In more recent years with the numbers of salmon declining, there has been less netting in the Dean Channel and as a result, returns of steelhead have been more consistent.

The number of anglers fishing the Dean has increased steadily since the first lodges were established on the upper river in the early to mid 60s. In the decade of the 80s, anglers fishing on their own increased dramatically. British Columbia's Ministry of the Environment installed a quota system in 1990 to control the situation. This was the first such restriction placed on a British Columbia stream. Other special streams in the

province may receive this designation in the years to come.

All non-guided, non-Canadian anglers wishing to fish the Dean and camp, as opposed to staying with a licensed operator, must secure an application and apply for a permit. You can write for an application to: Dean River Draw, Fisheries Management Branch, BC Fisheries, PO Box 9359 Stn Prov Govt, Victoria, British Columbia V8W 9M2. The application asks for specific dates in addition to a second choice of dates. The draw is conducted in March. After the draw, you can call (604/387-9587) to see if any spots are still available. If openings are available, you can make a reservation on the telephone. Anglers who stay at licensed camps are exempt from the draw. For information on the Internet, log on to: www.bcfisheries.gov.bc.ca/rec/fresh/dean/draw.html.

For those who are unfamiliar with the river, a few points should be noted. The stream is physically divided into three parts and these boundaries are also used to classify the water when issuing permits to anglers. Above Lake Anahim is trout water which is of no concern to us here. The lowest section below the gorge flows for two miles before emptying into salt water and is classified as Class II. Access to the lower river is easy because float planes land in the Dean Channel near the river's mouth and wheeled crafts can land on a nearby strip. Many anglers not staying in a licensed camp faithfully fish the lower river every year. Some of their campsites have been constantly improved and judging from their appearance, these sites are as comfortable a wilderness retreat as you can imagine.

Non-Canadians fishing the lower section need a $32.10 Basic License, a $42 Steelhead License, and a Class II License purchased at a cost of $10 for each day you fish. Even if you don't plan to keep any steelhead, you must purchase all three licenses to fish legally. The number of days that can be fished is eight. Not long ago, it was possible to fish this part of the Dean for as many days as you wished. Some chose to fish the river above the gorge for eight days and then would move down to fish the stream below. Now, though, non-Canadians are only allowed to fish a total of eight days on the Dean.

From the gorge, to the mouth of Craig Creek, in the section where the upper river lodges are located, is classified as Class I. This is the most productive stretch of the river. The lowest part of this section of the river, continuing to the runs well above the main lodges, can be expected to provide good fishing through mid September. The fishing does not become prime in the upper reaches of the river until concentrations of fish

Prime summer-run Steelhead have a silver/grey back and sides of pearl white. They are extremely strong swimmers as their reproductive organs are completely undeveloped and all the feeding at sea has been used to make them strong to endure months in the stream before they spawn. Dean River steelhead are known to feed while in the river making them extremely attracted to flies.

Anglers have been coming to the Dean for years to set camp next to the river below the gorge. From the looks of this camp, it is wilderness camping very refined.

begin arriving in the first part of August. However, some early fish do reach these waters in late July, but the timing of the runs is not the same each year. Non-Canadian anglers are limited to eight consecutive days of fishing annually.

In addition to the basic license and the steelhead license, you must buy a Class I License at a cost of $20 a day.

By the jurisdiction of the Ministry of Environment, there have been two licensed outfitters on the lower river in years past. Ordinarily, outfitters' licenses are distributed on the basis of the previous year's operation, but are annually reviewed to evaluate any changes.

Anglers at Moose Lake Lodge stay in two-person cabins located on a bluff overlooking the bay with spectacular views and are transported to the fishing by jet boat. The lodge takes six anglers with pairs of anglers sharing a guide. Guests normally stay for three days on the Dean as part of a package plan with the other fishing days of the week spent on other rivers for trout, such as the Blackwater. Prime weeks run from mid July to mid August. The lodge is about 1,000 feet from the airstrip.

Nakia Lodge, Box 306, Bella Coola, British Columbia, Canada V0T 1C0 (Vancouver Mobile Radio N-710611 Channel 2) is the other lower river lodge. Tony and Judy Hill were the original operators of this lodge. In 1993, after the season ended, Tony was killed in a boating accident. Judy passed all the outfitter license tests and was in full operation the following season with the help of a local guide and has since married Adam Tavener. Permanent bungalows house anglers, and a jet boat is used to transport anglers on the lower river.

When Chris and I visited the lodge in 1988, Judy cooked exceptional meals while Tony was able to provide transportation to and on the upper river. He drove his clients to the upper river by truck where he kept a jet boat. Since he did not have a guide's license for that stretch of river, he could only drop anglers off and then return to pick them up. This taxi service was also a boon to anglers camping on the river above the gorge as this was a convenient way to transport gear from the lower river.

Under these circumstances, Nakia's operation was only feasible for experienced anglers with the mobility to cover water on their own. The lodge still holds a permit to transport anglers to

A narrow gorge divides the upper Dean River from the lower. The steelhead move swiftly through the lower river and then must negotiate the fast flowing waters of the gorge to reach the upper river. This steep course denies fish not strong enough from reaching the spawning grounds making the Dean River steelhead one of the strongest anadromous fish in the world.

the river above the gorge, but the permit does not allow anglers to be placed on runs by boat as was previously the case. Anglers are driven on the old logging road on the north side of the river and dropped off at more productive pools. Many anglers who would like to fish the waters above the gorge without being able to secure a rod at one of the upper river lodges welcome this opportunity. When making reservations, an angler can request as many days of fishing as is desired on the upper river to fill out a week's fishing and will be charged accordingly.

Because the operation at Nakia Lodge offers a variety of services and accommodations, prices are set depending on where anglers want to fish and how much service they require. The lodge hosts eight anglers, and their season runs from June through September. Nakia arranges for complete trips emanating from Vancouver.

Anglers who fish the lower river must be aware that competition for the water can be intense at times because there are not many holding places for fish. If water levels are low enough to permit passage through the gorge, steelhead do not linger and move through rapidly. Even so, guided anglers can expect to have two to three hook-ups each day. Since the fish are so close to salt water, they are as prime as they will ever be.

Because these steelhead are acclimating from salt to fresh water, it is advantageous to know something about how fish react to tidal movement. Fish ordinarily move into the stream with the flooding tide. At the beginning of the transition, when the water is still low, fish can be seen as they move over the bar from salt to fresh water. You can nearly feel the excitement in these fish returning from their wanderings. They are usually very fickle steelhead difficult to entice, but you can track their movement and cast to them. When hooked, some rush down over the bar back into salt water so fast that anglers are unable to follow and the fish are often lost. Once the tide rises enough so the advancing steelhead can't be seen, they are no longer vulnerable. It becomes impossible to know where to cast a fly to intercept them. At this time, you must move upstream looking for areas that are shallow enough to expose moving fish. This fishing is only for those with experience in tracking fish, anglers capable of more than average casting skills. Once the steelhead move upstream beyond the influence of the tides, they act like the stream fish which many anglers are more familiar with.

Beginning in early June and through the first part of July, anglers on the lower river target the runs of king salmon. This is the most heavily fished time on the lower river, but there is a short lull between the main run of salmon and the major push of steelhead. From this in-between period, through mid August, is a prime time for steelhead on the lower river.

Reservations at the upper river lodges have always been in great demand. They have been made even more sought after since the decline of Atlantic salmon fishing on the East Coast. Since fishing for both Atlantic salmon and steelhead are comparable, many eastern anglers are heading west. Yet, anglers who fish from one of the upper river camps the previous year have the first option of returning in the following year. As a result, anglers wishing to fish from an upper river camp must first wait to gain a spot and then work up from less desirable times to more prime weeks. Once anglers have the weeks they prefer, they do not give them up easily.

Two licensed lodges on the upper river are Hodson's and Stewart's. (Stewart's was sold to a new owner just recently.) Hodson's, Box 397, Bella Coola, British Columbia V0T 1C0 (604/982-2322) hosts eight anglers. Six stay at the main lodge and two at a spike camp above Kalone Creek. Hodson's holds an exclusive guiding permit for the river above Kalone Creek, and an angler's week is Friday to Friday. If openings exist, the week can be split between the main lodge and the upper camp, but the cost of a stay does not include airfare from Vancouver. Hodson's main lodge is located about seven miles above the mouth, which places it about three miles above the top of the gorge.

Daryl Hodson, founder and owner of the lodge, was killed in a helicopter accident in 1991. Nancy, his wife, Jill and Danny, their daughter and son, and Jill's husband, Bob Hull, now run the lodge. Each three anglers are rotated between the guides. Meals are served to take the best advantage of the fishing day. Breakfast is served early and the main meal is served during midday when fish are usually less active. A light evening meal is taken on the river because this is often the best time to be fishing. Hodson's is open from late June through September 31.

Stewart's Camp, which was recently sold, is just a mile upstream from Hodson's. The lodges share the water on an amicable basis. There is never any conflict or competition for the water between visiting anglers. Stewart's fishes a total of twelve anglers, nine at the main lodge and three more at a camp below Kalone Creek. The spike camp opens later in the season after angling conditions become stable. The price for a stay varies depending if you stay five or seven days

and whether you choose the main lodge or the upper camp.

There are advantages to the upper river lodges. While the lower river summer-runs are essentially finished by mid August, the upper river fish are available through mid September. The first weeks of August are considered the most prime on the upper river as this is when the main thrust of the runs pass through. However, summer-run fish continue to move through the canyon of the Dean into the upper river through the first part of September. Though fewer in number, they augment the earlier arriving fish and provide for good fishing.

It is believed that the early arriving fish are more "hot" than those arriving later. With the combination of moderate water temperatures to promote dry-fly fishing, the freshness of the fish, and the most likely possibility of casting to the heaviest part of the run, it is no wonder that the first weeks of August are preferred.

The Dean above the gorge is as near perfect a steelhead river as you will find. Many of the runs are easily fished with a fly, providing the angler is a competent caster. The river valley has become a hallowed place for many with cathedral-like mountains rising above the banks. Huge log-jams, seemingly situated to make it difficult for anglers on foot to move from one pool to the next, make a boat used for transportation almost mandatory.

Guests at the upper river lodges are transported up and down the river by jet-driven boats and then fishing is done by wading. This mobility allows a good stretch of river to be fished for the best results.

For all the grand topography of its domain, the Dean River steelhead strain sets it apart from other steelhead by its inherent qualities. These fish are known for their aggressiveness, and at times, are known to attack the fly. At first light, some steelhead hold very near the bank. It is not unusual to find fish inside the current edge in nearly static water. At other times, they can be found close to the head of a run just where riffled waters start to flatten. Like steelhead waters anywhere, the tails of pools are notorious for holding fish. For experienced steelhead anglers, it seems that all the likely places that could hold fish often do.

In the early season, or when water levels are high, large flies are commonly used, but the patterns you choose don't seem to be important.

The summer-run steelhead of the Dean River are most receptive to flies presented in the early morning and then again at dusk, typical of all summer-run fish. When approaching the stream at first light, it is best to assume fish may be holding close to the shoreline before making presentations to deeper water.

The Dean River enters the Dean Channel near Kimsquit, a docking area where logs were once gathered to be shipped south.

Large fur or marabou leeches may work just as well as #2 Popsicles. The Popsicle is made by tying large bunches of fluorescent marabou in different colors. When the fly is wet, it looks somewhat like a Rainbow Popsicle. Through the course of a week's fishing, you may find use for many traditional steelhead patterns plus the waking fly of your choice. A steelhead Humpy has been a favorite.

The Inside Angler visited the Hodson camps in 1990 and 1991, with the first visit in the third week of September. Fishing was exclusively on the upper waters above Kalone Creek, which were made available to guests by using a helicopter each day. The fishing was very good and the two anglers landed 20 to 25 steelhead, each, for the week. That autumn was very warm and glacial melt discolored the water making fishing at the main lodge not nearly as productive as it would have been in cooler temperatures.

The upper river above Kalone Creek is much smaller than the river below. Two large tributaries enter the main river below Kalone Creek and are responsible for dirtying the water during heavy rains or warm glacial melt. This makes the upper river camp very desirable, especially later in the season when it holds increasingly larger numbers of steelhead.

In the following year, the fishing was done in the first week of August with time split between the water above Kalone Creek and the main lodge. The fish total for the lodge (8 rods) was 140 for the week. The count was almost equally divided between steelhead caught above Kalone Creek and below. It proved to be one of the best weeks of the season. The majority of the fish weighed between eight and thirteen pounds with some larger. All were bright fish without a trace of color. Compared to the steelhead caught the previous year later in the season, these early fish fought much harder and were airborne more frequently.

When I had the chance to visit the Dean and Nakia Lodge in 1988, it was a selfish undertaking. A group of anglers was formed by a travel company, which needed a group leader. I volunteered to be that person just for the opportunity to make a visit and did all I could to fulfill that obligation. With the exception of two anglers, however, the group had not fished for steelhead. Some could not even cast, so a day was set aside to provide some instruction prior to the trip. But all was for naught and our catch rate, as a group, was unimpressive. We fished the third week in July during a period following some rains and the river dropped in height and became clearer as each day passed. As might be expected, the fishing improved as the week progressed.

At the end of the stay, I had a most memorable day. Fishing in the morning and then again at dusk, I hooked ten, magnificent steelhead and landed seven, but part of my success could be attributed to my varied presentations. Fish were hooked on a Muddler fished dead drifted on a floating line. This same fly was fished more traditionally quartered across the current just barely breaking the surface on a floating line and it proved effective. A sink-tip line, delivering a Green Butted Skunk, deceived some fish after the floating line presentations had run their course. Several large steelhead, holding in faster and deeper water with king salmon, took a Silver Hilton fished on a High Density Shooting Taper. I fished with a #8 system and was glad I had brought along a full assortment of lines.

Because many anglers are financially unable to fish the Dean in the manner of the upper river lodges, like most everything else, there are ways to make a trip possible with certain tradeoffs. For the entire month of August, during the peak of the runs, there is a boat ban on that portion of river directly upstream of the gorge for three kilometers. This allows campers to fish these choice runs without competition, except from other campers. This is not new and some groups have been coming during this period for many years. If this strikes your fancy, be forewarned that this is wilderness existence without any recourse if you should encounter any complications. If all your food is lost to bears, there is no place at hand to replace it.

This region is renown for its brown bears. If you happen to see any black bears and they do not flee at your coming, this would be unusual. Black bears are usually killed by the browns and run when seeing any large mammals. Black bears are more of a problem for campers who choose to fish higher on the river. An example of this was brought to my attention when talking to a couple of anglers who had camped and fished the upper river one September. Black bears became such a nuisance that the fishermen chose to leave early with time remaining on their permits. One of the anglers said, "they just got the best of me."

I spent a day with some campers on the section above the gorge and they seemed to be well prepared. After each meal, the cooking and eating area was cleared of all food. All uneaten food was secured inside an ice chest strung high in the trees on cables. Even their toothpaste was kept out of the sleeping tent as was everything else that could throw a scent. In addition to firecrack-

Erv Erlick makes ready to fish the river above the gorge. Large trees downed by the river's flow often gather to form logjams. These formidable barriers can be twenty feet high making it impossible to follow hooked fish that choose to race downstream evading capture.

ers, cherry bombs and sidearms, they had a high caliber rifle too. Every chore that was needed to maintain a scent-free camp was completed without delay. When one of them caught a salmon to be used for camp fare, it was quickly cleaned and cut into pieces small enough to fit into zip-locked bags. These, in turn, were put into larger zip-locked bags, a gunny sack, and then placed in the river anchored by some very large rocks. I saw them later in the week, and they had no problems. These were wilderness campers of some experience. Since this writing it is now catch and release only for steelhead.

Although the Dean has only been fished on an organized basis for less than 40 years, a strong tradition has developed. Anglers are indebted to the foresight of the founders of the original lodges on the upper river. It was their wish after discovering the uniqueness of the Dean, that the wild state of the river and all that comes with this should somehow be preserved, though, there is no doubt that the manner in which anglers are selected to fish the upper river has brought about a certain controversy. For some, it may seem inequitable, but ground rules have been established and are followed by everyone. Those who are persistent will eventually gain prime spots on the river. Along the way, they will be dealt less than the best slots, but this is not an uncommon occurrence. For many years now, these lodges did not need or even wish to advertise the river as a destination and they still don't. For anglers who may want to fish the Dean River, where there is the will, there is a way.

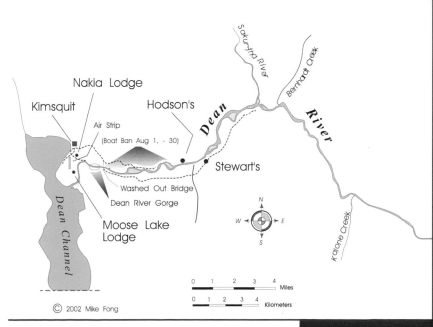

© 2002 Mike Fong

DEAN RIVER

EAGLE LAKE

3 Northeast California

EAGLE LAKE

O ne of the greatest successes of the California Department of Fish and Game was to bring back the indigenous Eagle Lake rainbow from the brink of extinction. It's a story that has been told many times before, but because it is so significant, worth telling again. The highly alkaline waters of Eagle Lake near Susanville in Modoc County were thought to be devoid of trout. In the 50s, a few pair of breeding rainbows were found in Pine Creek by Spaulding, the only development on the lake. From these few trout, the Department of Fish & Game started a program where they trapped spawning fish each spring, raised their young in a hatchery and released them back into the lake. The replanted rainbows quickly grew fat on the abundant leeches, scud and the native tui chub minnows. It wasn't long thereafter that anglers began catching trophy size fish. The fishing that this ongoing program sustains makes Eagle Lake one of the best, if not the best, fishing lake in the Golden State for trophy-size rainbows.

As mentioned in our report in Volume II, Number 4, July 1993, the Eagle Lake rainbow has been used throughout the West to rejuvenate failing fisheries. It has become the fish of choice among managers responsible for providing fishing in waters where there was only mediocre or poor sport. Eagle Lake rainbows are highly resistant to disease and adapt to streams on lakes. Since the published report, Chris and I have caught Eagle Lake rainbows in the North Platte River near Alcova in Wyoming, Georgetown Lake in Montana, the Green River below Fontenelle Reservoir in Wyoming, in the Madison River in Yellowstone National Park, in Hebgen Lake itself, in Davis Lake in Oregon and many waters in California. They have been tempted to the surface to take dry flies, taken nymphs when they chose to feed below the surface and were caught on streamers and Woolly Buggers.

The author hooks up after seeing a fish disturb the surface and making a cast to lead the fish before beginning a slow retrieve with a leech pattern.

The author walks down a beach looking for signs of fish moving in the shallows. Even in low light, movement of fish can be seen if anglers watch closely.

earnest. Filming the opening could wait. There wasn't even enough time to don waders. In just a few casts, I hooked a rainbow, landed it and we had it all on film. As I recall, this sequence is not seen on the final cut. We had such good fishing for the remainder of the day that this footage was never used.

The first time Chris and I came to fish Eagle Lake was in early June of 1982. We knew nothing about the fishing and called a sporting goods store in Susanville for information. This store was mentioned frequently in fishing reports coming from Eagle Lake. The proprietor was a flyfisher named Jack Roberts and his shop was the Sportsman. He kindly offered to fish with us one morning to show us what he could.

On Eagle Lake, you rarely see fish rising to the surface to take a food item. That doesn't mean you won't see some kind of disturbance on the surface because they often roll on top when moving from one feeding area to another. Eagle Lake rainbows are frequently found in very shallow water by tules in search of minnows. When an attack is made on the baitfish, it often results in commotion on the surface. This is one of the most obvious signs to look for when fishing Eagle Lake.

One late October morning while filming a segment at Eagle Lake for the "Charles West's Outdoor Gazette" television program, I prepared to do the "opening." For these segments, I scripted the beginning, middle, and the closing. The rest of the footage came from whatever fishing we encountered during the day. Through the years, there were only two destinations where we didn't catch fish. Still, this possibility always loomed large and there was a lot of anxiety until the first fish was in the "can." The place I selected to introduce the segment was a point of land that jutted into the lake. A breeze blowing from the south created a lee to the left of the point, that attracted a large school of tui chub. As I spoke to the camera lens, there was the unmistakable sound of a predator fish attacking baitfish behind me. If this was a singular event, I might have dismissed it, but it soon became clear that more than one rainbow was starting to feed in

We arrived late in the afternoon of the preceding day. Walking through the door to his shop was like entering another time. From the ceiling hung model airplanes covered with dust, the kind that only comes with age. The fins of fish mounts had grown brittle and the feathers of the waterfowl and fur of animals had long since lost their sheen. Some items in his display cases attracted my attention. In their original boxes were lures no longer produced used to fish for largemouth bass and a variety of other fish. I'm not a collector, but I had to purchase some. There were some Voo Doo lures made by the Voo Doo Lure Company in San Francisco long ago. They were deadly for steelhead on the Russian River. I had heard of them, but had never seen one of these jointed lures that look kind of like a Lazy Ike. I had to have some of the Flatfish and Russelures because the boxes were marked to be used especially with fly rods. What was even more amazing was that the original prices were still on the boxes. Rick had a young lad still in high school helping in the shop and he waited on us. His name was Andy Burke. As I'm sure many of you already know, Andy has become one of the most innovative fly tiers in the West and an angler with a growing reputation.

For those who are unfamiliar with the fishing at Eagle Lake, my advice is to fish shallow when the water temperatures is 63 degrees or less. In the spring, this means from June through early July.

Flyfishing during the summer slows as fish find comfort near deep-water springs. When the water cools with the coming of fall, fish again head for the shallows. At first, they are only present at first light and at dusk. Once autumn moves into early winter, the shallows of Eagle Lake may hold fish throughout the day. Depending on the year, the water level may vary tremendously. When it's high enough, there can be water deep enough to hold fish inside the stand of tules that line many shore areas. Before I stumbled onto these fish, very few anglers knew they were vulnerable and even fewer fished for them. A sequence explained in the report will give you a better understanding of a technique that I found productive for these rainbows. For the stillwater angler, a visit to Eagle Lake is highly recommended. The lake closes to fishing on December 31, when the upper end of the lake may be completely frozen over. Prepare for extremely cold weather if planning a visit any time after Thanksgiving. It's a strange experience to be fishing a part of the lake where the water is open and hear, from other parts of the lake, sheets of ice grinding against each other like the hum of automobile traffic on some distant freeway.

EAGLE LAKE

The rainbow trout of Eagle Lake in California is unique. There is still some question as to whether this fish is properly designated as a rainbow because it's found in a region originally dominated by cutthroat. Owing to its evolution in alkaline water, it has developed a resistance to many diseases that affect other fish. It grows quickly to large size with a penchant for eating smaller fish and has large teeth to utilize the large population of minnows in its native water. Its diet is not restricted to small minnows, as it will also eat aquatic insects, crustaceans and other invertebrates with equal enthusiasm. Known mainly as a fish dwelling in a lake, it adapts easily to a stream. Because of these qualities, the Eagle Lake rainbow is a fish culturist's dream. This special rainbow has been introduced into waters throughout the West where indigenous and other introduced species have not sustained themselves. For example, a stretch of the North Platte River in Wyoming has a thriving population of Eagle Lake rainbows. They have also been planted in Hebgen Lake in Montana. Where the fall migration of brown trout was once the main focus for anglers

fishing the Madison River in Yellowstone Park, a large number of Eagle Lake rainbows now join them. In years to come, the Eagle Lake rainbow may be used to rejuvenate other waters of the West where fishing has deteriorated. Still, Eagle Lake remains the most reliable place to catch this indigenous rainbow.

Eagle Lake lies in the semi-arid, northeast corner of California about fifteen miles north of Susanville. At 5,100 feet above sea level, the air temperature ranges from around 100 degrees in August to near zero in the dead of winter. The lake is divided into three distinct parts, each oval in shape. The northern part has an average depth of six feet. There is a public boat launch at Stones Landing where the Mariner's Resort is located. This complex has a restaurant, lounge, and general store with fishing tackle, RV Park and boat rental service. We found the facilities well maintained and the bathhouses very clean. While the complex is open all season, the restaurant/bar is only open from Memorial Day to Labor Day.

Divided from the upper part of the lake by Duck Point, the mid section is slightly deeper with an average depth of ten feet. On the western shoreline at mid lake lies Spaulding Tract, the only major development on the lake comprised of private homes and commercial businesses. The Osprey Inn was completed in 1994 and is the most recently built accommodations in the area. Close by is Lakeview Inn, which has motel rooms, a store, a restaurant and boat rental service. The rooms are small, but clean. We found the food well prepared at the restaurant with the kitchen offering anglers a special service where the cook prepares your catch and serves it with all the trimmings. The Eagle Lake rainbow is delicious with firm, flaky, pink meat. Since the lake receives a plant of 150,000 fish each year, the population remains stable regardless of harvest. In some years, many of the fish planted are of the neutered variety. They may grow to trophy size even faster than the regular plants. The limit imposed on anglers is two fish daily with four in possession. Adult fish are trapped each spring at the mouth of Pine Creek, just north of Spaulding Tract. The young are raised at Crystal Lake Hatchery next to Baum Lake. Surplus fish from Baum, in addition to the production from two other hatcheries, are used for planting in other waters.

For those with private airplanes, there is a 4640-foot paved landing strip at Spaulding Tract. The Eagle Lake RV Park is located two blocks east of Lakeview Inn and offers a variety of accommo-

Woolly Buggers in different colors can be used to imitate the leeches in the lake as well as some of the minnows.

A big rainbow takes the author's scud imitation as it is retrieved next to some cattails.

provisions are stocked at the store. There are showers; tokens purchased at the store are needed to operate them. The telephone number of the marina is (916/825-3454) should you need to contact them.

Four campgrounds are located at the south end of the lake. Reservations through the Mistix system (1/800/283-CAMP) are required for camping at Eagle Campground. For $12/night, picnic tables, fire pits and flush toilets are provided at Eagle Campground. Campsites at Merrill Campground cost $12/night. The campsites at Christie Campgrounds are mostly away from the water and the charge is $10/night. It costs $8 for a site at Aspen, which is restricted to tent camping. The campgrounds close in December.

Water temperatures in Eagle Lake dip to 32 degrees in winter and rise to nearly 80 degrees in summer. For flyfishers, this is critical as fish are not as likely to be found in the shallows or near the surface once the surface water temperature exceeds 63 degrees. This means that the best flyfishing takes place when the lake is opened to fishing on the Saturday nearest Memorial Day, and normally lasts until mid July. In mid July, the surface water temperature, rises above the critical mark and trout are only found in the shallows very early in the morning and at dusk. From mid July on, as the water warms, the rainbows retreat to the sanctuary of submerged springs.

In October, the surface water temperature drops below sixty-three degrees and the trout return to the shallows. From this time on, until the lake closes to fishing on December 31, is another

dations. These include cabins, a studio apartment, mobile homes and trailers, all with fully equipped kitchens and color television. Depending on the unit, some come with bedding while for others, this is charged as an extra. Prices vary with the choice of accommodations. Reservations should be made well ahead of time, especially during holiday weekends. On these three-day weekends, a two-day minimum stay is required. Rates for tent camping sites and full RV hookups are reasonable.

Pelican Point is the name of the peninsula separating the mid part of the lake from the deepest part at the southern end. Nearly ninety feet deep, fish winter in this part of the lake. From north to south, the lake covers thirteen miles and is four miles at its widest point. Growing along the shoreline in many places are stands of tules. These can extend out into the lake creating channels that fish use to migrate inshore looking for minnows. Lacking tules, the rest of the shoreline is nearly barren with sagebrush growing to the water's edge. However, tall trees can be found at the southern end of the lake creating shade for summer campers at one of the four campgrounds and at a few other isolated spots around the lake. The first dirt road west of Christie Campground leads to Wildcat Point. This is the only automobile access to this part of the lake. Car-top boats can be launched here. I have found fishing along the shoreline to the north more productive than to the south.

At the southern end of the lake, there is a marina, boat launch and general store. There is no charge to use the multi-ramp boat launch. Gas for boats can be purchased at the dock and

During the night, clouds began to build and when we started to fish in the morning, the sky looked like it was on fire.

prime time to flyfish the lake. From year to year, the weather patterns change. On the average, the best months to fish Eagle with a fly rod are June, early July, October and November. However, during years when the weather is mild, December can be good too. Chris and I have had some of our best fishing in the last month of the year. The upper and mid parts of the lake start to freeze over as winter arrives and the boat launches at Stone's Landing and at Spaulding Tract close. Since the most productive flyfishing takes place when the trout are in the shallows or near the surface, this just about puts an end to flyfishing regardless of the official date of closing.

Although the best flyfishing is done when fish are near the surface or in shallow water, this does not mean that good fishing only comes to those who wade to fish. A boat is needed to reach many of the more productive places. The entire lake bottom is rock and rubble. Shallow shoals are unmarked and even experienced boaters carry extra shear pins. Be very careful when boating on the lake.

Until the spring of 2001, Jay Fair was the only flyfishing guide on the lake. He resided in Spaulding, but has since moved back to Portola. Jay still guides on Eagle Lake and charges $125/person with a two-angler minimum. I've known Jay for more than thirty years. When we first met, he was on the Fish and Game Commission in Portola County. Jay is seventy-nine years old. As long as I've known him, he has always been a fly fisherman. Clients fish mainly from his boat, but wading may be done as well. A typical day consists of an early start motoring to a point or bay that he suspects holds fish. Provided you are a capable caster, you might wade to cover

the spot then board the boat to try another location. Notice that the places you fish will have a bottom of rubble, rocks and gravel. This is the preferred habitat for Gammarus (scud) and leeches, both important foods for Eagle Lake rainbows. The water is clear and it's easy to distinguish this fertile bottom from the clean, sterile, pavement-like bottom, which does not attract trout.

Since you will be fishing shallow water or near the surface, a #5 or #6 system with a weight-forward floating or intermediate line is used. A ten-foot leader with a six-pound-test tippet is recommended. Jay relies primarily on his own leech patterns, which can also pass for a minnow. If the fish are not on the points or in the bays, he will often anchor the boat the distance of a long cast off a point between two bays that are known to attract feeding fish. As the fish move from feeding area to feeding area, they often swim near the surface with one occasionally rolling on top. The Eagle Lake rainbow is gregarious and often swims in small groups. Because of this, when a fish is hooked and more than one angler is in a boat, the other angler should continue casting. If this strategy is employed, double hook ups are not uncommon. Throughout the day, Jay may have you try a number of places between feeding areas, hoping to intercept fish. As evening approaches, he will position you on a point or in a bay as the fish frequent these places during low light conditions.

Ordinarily, the most productive climactic situation in autumn and early winter on Eagle Lake is during threatening weather. An overcast day without wind and a hint of winter on the way is just perfect. Under these conditions, a pair of competent anglers fishing with Jay might hook as many as twenty-five rainbows running anywhere from a pound and a half to eight or nine pounds. The greatest majority will weigh between two and three pounds. Since it can get cold this time of year, and rain is a strong possibility, dress warmly. Chris and I wear boot-footed neoprene waders over layered clothing. A reliable rain jacket can be used for double duty as a windbreaker. If it rains, you are prepared. An item we find indispensable is a pair of gloves. Neoprene is a good material, but I prefer a pair of heavy-duty latex gloves worn over a pair of heavy wool gloves. The advantage of latex gloves is that they go further up the arm so when handling a fish in the water, your hands remain dry. Even with neoprene gloves, it's hard to keep your hands warm once they get wet in cold weather. Using the combination of gloves to remain warm is something I learned from fishing for winter steelhead in inclement weather.

Most of the rainbows in Eagle Lake are planted, but a few are born in the only stream that flows into the lake, like this one.

With Jay being the only flyfishing guide on the lake, you should book early to guarantee some time. If you want to purchase his unique flies or the material he uses to make them, these can be ordered directly from Jay.

Many anglers prefer to fish on their own from prams, canoes, belly boats, or to wade. All these approaches can be productive. With a pram or canoe, you are able to cover more water than by wade fishing. With such a craft, you are not limited to using a launch ramp. I often use a pram because I can stand and see into the water for a distance. This may not be a safe practice so if you do the same, be sure to wear a lifesaving device. Many places, like the flats off the air strip at Spaulding Tract, hold fish in water less than three feet deep provided the water temperature reaches the comfort level of the trout. This area extends from the launch ramp east as far as Pelican Point. You can either put in your portable boat from the launch ramp, from the narrow, dirt road at the beginning of the airstrip or from the end of the road fronting the airstrip. If you choose the latter, it will require carrying your craft about fifty yards depending on the level of the lake.

Many of the fish I see on this flat are singles. They are either cruising slowly as if looking for food, corralling minnows gathered off points or stands of tules, or lying in shallow depressions. When seen chasing minnows, the trout are focused and not as likely to be frightened when approached. Cast to cover the area where the trout is feeding and retrieve your leech with short strips hoping the rainbow sees it.

When fishing water less than thigh deep in my pram, I stand and use an oar as a pole. This allows me a much better angle to see into the water. As I push the pram along, I scan the water ahead. This can be done with a canoe as well. Move slowly and quietly and you will often see trout just holding still. Many times, a clump of tules will obstruct your cast and if the wind is blowing, you might not be able to change your course without alarming the trout. A number of times, I've flushed an unsighted trout and watched hopelessly as it swam away. Surprisingly, the trout will often swim only a short distance and then turn around. Even more surprising is that some will often take a #6 Sheep Creek if it's cast to land delicately in its vicinity and retrieved slowly. The only time this sight-fishing is possible is during midday when you can easily see into the water. Polarized glasses are a great aid in helping to see fish.

In early morning before sunrise and at dusk, fish can be found in water less than knee deep. This water is mainly inside the tule line between the shore and standing vegetation. For these fish, it's advantageous to wade. In order to do this safely and effectively, you must look at these places during the day to see if any deeper pockets pose a problem. At the same time you are looking for problem wading areas, you should be looking for areas fish seem to frequent. If fish are found in particular places during the day, it's highly likely they will be there during first light.

I like to be on the water as soon as it's light enough to see where I'm wading. Most often, there is no wind and the surface will show the slightest movement of fish. Once in a while, a swirl will give away the location of a trout, but the signs are usually very subtle. For instance, a trout turning to chase a minnow will push water away from the direction it swims. This is the kind of sign you must interpret. Many times, you need to rely on your senses to direct your cast. Cast short to a suspected trout rather than overcasting on the first presentation. If your first cast does not attract the fish, you will get another chance. If you cast beyond the fish on the first presentation, the disturbance made by the landing line will frighten the rainbow away and you will lose any chance of catching it.

Sometimes, you find fish cruising in the open away from the tules. A greater percentage of the time, the trout will hold very close to the tules as this is where minnows hide. Once I cover all the water I can by wading up to my knees, I make probing casts up alleys between lanes of tules. For this wade fishing, use a tippet of ten-pound test. Hooked fish swim into and around tules and the only chance you have of landing them is to use some muscle. Luckily, trout are not leader shy. My fly of choice for this wade fishing is a #6 Sheep Creek tied on a 1x strong hook. This fishing can be compared to fishing for bonefish on dark days, however the fishing on Eagle Lake is a bit easier because the fish are not constantly on the move. Because the trout are almost stationary, proceed slowly and watch for the slightest water movement. Once you find some success with this wade-fishing technique, you might find it very interesting and fun.

After the first precipitation of autumn combines with the first freezing temperatures, the road from Susanville on the west side of the lake to reach Spaulding Tract can become icy. The ice can be of the black variety and impossible to see when driving. You stand a better chance of avoiding the ice by arriving at the lake in the afternoon instead of morning. Be sure to call ahead to see if black ice has formed. If black ice has formed, take the road on the east side of the lake to reach

One of the reasons why Eagle Lake rainbows grow so rapidly is a plentiful food supply. This is the underside of a flat rock taken from a shallow bay showing the amount of scuds that can cluster together.

Spaulding Tract. It will take a bit more driving time, but ice is less of a problem.

You might also encounter fog. If the forecast is for fair weather, the fog will burn off by late morning. Sometimes it lingers for days making driving hazardous. When fishing in the shallows under a blanket of fog, be aware that the duck hunting season opens on November 15, and hunters like to set their decoys out on the points. It can be unnerving when the loud report of a shotgun goes off and you are not expecting it. Pelican Point off Spaulding Tract and Buck Point are popular places for hunters. You might steer clear of these areas when the season is in progress. The duck hunting season in California is normally set in August. Check with the Department of Fish & Game for the exact dates of the season.

In recent years, more and more flyfishers are discovering the excellent sport on Eagle Lake. Some flyfishing clubs now plan annual outings in the fall. The nearest commercial airport is located in Reno where rental cars are available. An autumn trip to this area might include a trip to Pyramid Lake as well. Pyramid Lake is "the place" to catch a trophy cutthroat.

As the sun just begins to rise, Jay Fair nets a rainbow for Chris.

Eagle Lake rainbows come inshore to forage when the water temperature in the shallows is in the low 60s or lower. Anglers can recognize feeding areas by an irregular bottom covered with detritus where scud and leeches are plentiful. In order not to spook fish by motoring too close, it is best to wade within casting range of these rainbows feeding in the shallows before casting.

SUMMARY

Eagle Lake remains one of the best trophy-trout lakes in California. For the flyfisher, the lake is most productive when surface water temperatures are in the low 60s or lower, attracting trout into the shallows. The prime times to fish are from the opening on the Saturday nearest Memorial Day to mid July, and then again from mid October to the season ending on December 31. Having a boat is advantageous not only for transportation, but for anchoring and fishing points often used by the trout as they move from one feeding area to another. In the low light of early morning and at dusk, expect to find fish in the shallows in water less than three or four feet deep. During overcast days and during inclement weather, some fish can be found in the shallows all day.

A subtle movement of water by some standing cattails catches the author's attention and the stalk begins.

Businesses

For a complete listing of businesses, contact the LASSEN COUNTY CHAMBER OF COMMERCE, 84 North Lassen Street, Susanville, CA 96130, Tel. 530-257-4323. Although businesses important to anglers are located around the lake, all mailing addresses are listed as being in Susanville. The Chamber has a website at www.lassencountychamber.org, but it doesn't lists specific businesses, as yet.

• JAY FAIR, P.O. Box 1035 Portola, CA 96122 Tel. 530-832-0828, fax 530-832-0728, toll free 877-680-3474, e-mail:ljfair@gbis.com, website: www.eagleflyfishing.com. EAGLE LAKE FLY FISHING, in addition to guiding sells premium fly-tying materials and flies.

• EAGLE LAKE GENERAL STORE, 503-150 Mahogany Way, Susanville, CA 96130; Tel 530-825-2191, is located in Spaulding and has provisions for visiting anglers.

• MARINERS RESORT, STONES LANDING, Susanville, CA 96130; Tel. 530-825-3333, 1-800-700-5253 is located at the north side of the lake. This complex has a restaurant, lounge, and general store with fishing tackle, RV Park and boat rental service. For camping and no hook ups, the charge is $9.50/day. For full RV hookup, it's $25/day. While the complex is open all season, the restaurant/bar is only open from Memorial Day to Labor Day. mariners@citlink.net

• LAKEVIEW INN, 502-845 The Strand, Susanville, CA 96130; Tel. 530-825-3555 is located at Spaulding. It has motel rooms, a store, a restaurant and rents boats. The rooms are small, clean and go for $45-85/night. We found food well prepared at the restaurant with the kitchen offering anglers a special service. For $10.95 a person, the cook prepares your catch with all the trimmings. A specialty was baking the fish, which was thenserved whole on a platter. E-mail: info@eaglelakeresort.com

• THE EAGLE LAKE RV PARK, 687-125 Palmetto Way, Spaulding Tract, Susanville, CA 96130; Tel. 530-825-3133, is located two blocks east of Lakeview Inn. It is situated in a grove of pine trees and has campsites, hot showers, RV hookups, game room and a variety of accommodations. These include cabins, a studio apartment, mobile homes and trailers. All have fully-equipped kitchens with microwave ovens, and color television. The mobile home even has a VCR. Depending on the unit, some come with bedding while for others, this is charged as an extra. Prices vary, with the rate of a travel trailer starting at $35/day. The 3-bedroom cabins can sleep up to six people and the rate is $125/day. Reservations

for these units should be made well ahead of time, especially during holiday weekends. On these three-day weekends, a two-day minimum stay is required. For tent camping sites, the rate is $12/day. Full RV hookup is $16/day and it is $14 for water and electricity.

At the southern end of the lake, there is a marina, boat launch and general store. There is no charge to use the multi-ramp boat launch. Gas for boats can be purchased at the dock and provisions are stocked at the store. There are showers, tokens purchased at the store are needed to operate them. The telephone number of the marina is 530-825-3454 should you need to contact them.

Jay Fair, a local guide on Eagle Lake, nets a rainbow for the author.

Camping

Four campgrounds are located at the south end of the lake. Reservations through the Mistix system. Tel. 1-800-283-CAMP are required for camping at Eagle Campground. For $12/night, picnic tables, fire pits and flush toilets are provided at Eagle Campground. Campsites at Merrill Campground costs $12/night. There are a few sites along the shore, but no trees for shade. The campsites at Christie Campgrounds are mostly away from the water and the charge is $10/night. It costs $8 for a site at Aspen, which is restricted to tent camping. The campgrounds close in December.

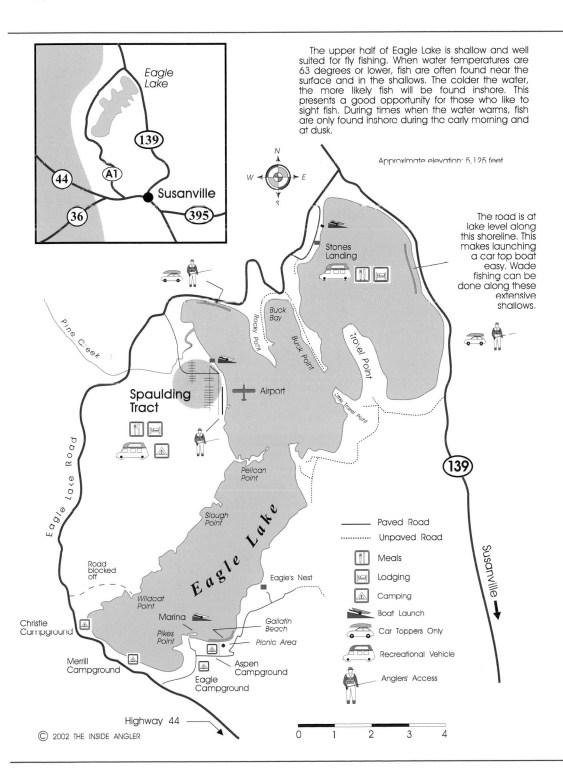

The upper half of Eagle Lake is shallow and well suited for fly fishing. When water temperatures are 63 degrees or lower, fish are often found near the surface and in the shallows. The colder the water, the more likely fish will be found inshore. This presents a good opportunity for those who like to sight fish. During times when the water warms, fish are only found inshore during the early morning and at dusk.

Approximate elevation: 5,125 feet

The road is at lake level along this shoreline. This makes launching a car top boat easy. Wade fishing can be done along these extensive shallows.

© 2002 THE INSIDE ANGLER

ELK RIVER

4 Alberta, Canada

ELK RIVER

A question that sometimes stops me cold is, "Where can I take a beginning angler fishing for wild trout so success is almost guaranteed?" Several possibilities come to mind and the Elk River in Alberta would have to be rated near or at the top of the list. One of our subscribers went to the Elk after our report on the river was filed because he wanted to introduce his young son to flyfishing. The trip was an overwhelming success. Not only did his son catch a good number of cutthroat on dry flies, but his mother-in-law, who at the time had never even flyfished, caught some too. They were in the care of a competent guide.

Of all the roadside rivers Chris and I have fished, the Elk is one of the most beautiful. It flows from north to south along the eastern front of the Canadian Rockies for more than forty trout-filled miles. If you turned your head away from the highway, you could easily envision yourself being miles from pavement. But in this case, the road is not a bad thing. The river's course is such that it winds away from the road for some distance and then returns. This it does repeatedly for many miles making it practical to drift short sections where on many rivers, once you commit to a drift, it can be a very long day. On many rivers, long drifts are necessary because trout populations are not dense and what trout that reside in the streams are spread widely.

Currently, the numbers of cutthroat in the Elk are near an all-time high. In 1995, just three years prior to our report in 1998, the Elk experienced an extremely severe winter. It got so cold, anchor ice formed and during the spring flood, the river bottom was scoured taking along with it most of the cutthroat trout. To allow the cutthroat population to recover, a no-kill policy was enacted. In two years, the cutthroat made a phenomenal comeback. Prior to the devastation, the trout population was strong, but with a certain amount of har-

Several times during our day with John, Chris and I had double hook ups with cutthroat. After landing these fish, John oared back upstream and we had another double.

vest allowed, the fishing could only be rated good. Presently, the numbers of cutthroat that can be landed in one day by two experienced anglers fishing with a good guide could surpass the century mark. There is a possibility that limited harvest on certain sections of the river may be allowed again, but that has not happened up to this point. Even if this was to be, I doubt if the overall quality of the fishery would be impacted. If this was a concern, you could always fish a section where the fish were fully protected.

To experience the best of what the Elk can offer, anglers should be on hand after run-off from snow melt is completed. In 1998 and 1999, there were circumstances that made the river high and roiled until the first week of August. Once the river drops and clears, it's possible to fish dry flies exclusively. A good idea is to fish two dries with the second fly tied on a dropper from the hook of the first. Hooking two fish on the same cast is a possibility. For two guided anglers to be hooked up to cutthroat simultaneously is more than likely. The Elk also hosts a fair population of bull trout (Dolly Varden), which are protected and must be released if caught. These carnivores are best tempted with a streamer or Woolly Bugger type fly. Three- to five-pound fish are typical. Bull trout larger than ten pounds are a possibility.

Not all of our subscribers hire guides. Some own their own boats and many more own personal inflatables that can be used safely on running water. There are raft types, like the Water Master, and pontoon types, such as the Outcast. Either type would be perfectly suited to the Elk as there are no dangerous rapids. Any serious threats from drifting would come from fallen trees obstructing passage. Anyone considering a drift should check with local businesses for current information. If you fish the stream near the town of Fernie, you should drop into the Kootenai Fly Shop for this information. They do shuttles and if you don't have a boat or inflatable and want to fish on your own, the shop has different kinds of crafts for rent.

The American dollar continues to be very strong in Canada. If the good fishing on the Elk and the strength of the dollar isn't

Under overcast skies, the author brings a cutthroat to hand. In the background by the highway are businesses at the southern part of Fernie.

The Elk River is one of British Columbia's most productive cutthroat streams. Highway 3 follows the river for most of its length.

enough to lure you across the border, consider that if you are in Missoula, it's only a drive of about four hours to reach Fernie. In this short time, you will be transported to a different angling world. Left behind is all that competition for the water that a stream as productive as the Elk in the United States would bring. It's a feeling so rare that most western trout anglers have forgotten what this is like.

ELK RIVER

After Jim Crawford, a long-time friend of ours, fished the St. Mary and Elk rivers in July 1998, he suggested that Chris and I should make a visit to southeast British Columbia to sample fishing in this area yet to be discovered by the angling masses. During his visit, the water was high from the record snow pack of the

the other, rock bars were exposed by low flows so typical of a western river late in the season.

By the time we reached the town of Fernie, where we met with Guide John Kendall, the wind had subsided even more. After having breakfast at the Cedar Lodge Restaurant and making a stop at the Kootenay Fly Shop, only opened for business the season before, the wind had just about died. John asked us which part of the river we wanted to drift and we told him to take us down the section most heavily floated. This would be from the north end of town down to the entrance to the Fernie Ski Resort, where there is an unimproved launch ramp. The reason for this choice was that we wanted to judge the quality of the fishing in this stretch compared to other sections less fished and to see how many anglers we would encounter on a weekend day. By the time we did the shuttle and began our drift, it was around noon.

John works for Josten, the company that specializes in producing school yearbooks, and guides part-time for Kelly Laatsch of Columbia River Outfitters (since changed to St. Mary Angler Flyshop). The last time he was on the Elk was two weeks earlier when the river was flowing at least eighteen inches higher. To give us some recent history on the Elk, John told about the tremendous flood in 1995. It was feared that following the flood, the trout population would be at an all-time low. To allow the cutthroat to repopulate the river, a two-year no-kill moratorium was imposed on the Elk. This moratorium was to end with the completion of the 1997 season and for the 1998 season, there would be sections still observing the no-kill regulations and some open to limited harvest. Most everyone was surprised to learn how fast the cutthroat population rebounded and how rapidly the fish grew as the moratorium approached the end of its second season. Because of an article published in Fly Fisherman Magazine, which mentioned the Elk River, angling

By autumn, the Elk is low and clear making the fishing of dry flies an effective method. There are few rapids, but anglers boating the river must be cautious as trees often obstruct the flow.

preceding winter and fishing was most productive when employing nymphs. In the low water of autumn a couple of months later, we found that dry flies provided all the action we could want on the Elk River.

On an early Sunday morning in mid September, Chris and I drove north from Polson, Montana crossing the border and arrived at Elko, British Columbia in about three hours. The wind was howling down the canyon where we saw the Elk River for the first time. It certainly didn't look promising as far as fishing was concerned. As we headed further north on Highway 3, the river valley began to widen and the wind started to diminish. At short distances from one another, there were pull-offs on the highway allowing access to the stream. These were perfect places where those with cartop boats or inflatables could launch to make short drifts. We stopped a couple of times to take photographs because as far as roadside rivers go, the Elk is one of the most beautiful. The highway runs along the base of mountains, that rise high on the west side of the river, and pastoral farmlands lie to the east. Trees lined the banks and alternating from one side to

John shows a nice bull trout before releasing it.

After handing my rod to John, I photographed Chris and John landing cutthroat simultaneously.

down the barbs of the hooks of our flies and wouldn't even set the hook unless the cutthroat was sizable. From one pool, Chris and I had three double hook ups. This was made possible because after hooking a couple of fish, John oared us back to the top of the pool two more times so we could fish the water again. Up till this time, we used hopper patterns exclusively. Just to experiment, I tied on a #14 Adams Paradun and landed two cutthroat in quick order. There were a few PMDs on the water plus a scattering of other aquatic insects, but never did we see anything resembling a sustained hatch. Since the hopper was easier to see, I soon went back to it.

The water temperature in the late afternoon was 55 degrees and the air temperature a pleasant twenty degrees higher. Unlike the first half of our drift, fish started to rise regularly in the afternoon. Once the fish became keyed on feeding, it was almost impossible to keep them from taking our flies. A couple of times, two cutthroats attacked my fly simultaneously. I laughed as things such as this don't happen to me that often.

Near the end of the drift, John joined us in the fun. He landed an eighteen-inch bull trout, which took a bead head nymph. This close cousin to the Dolly Varden grows to more than ten pounds in the Elk and is fully protected. Each one caught must be released unharmed. Before we began fishing this particular pool, John said it was one of his favorites in this section of river. Where the riffle entered, Chris landed another bull trout on a submerged hopper. This one weighed around four pounds. Thinking there might be a monster lurking in the depths, I switched to a sinking-

pressure had recently risen dramatically. Most of the increase resulted from independent anglers coming from the States, as you would expect, but the number of guides had risen substantially too. This growth in angler use created a controversy between local anglers, who previously had the river to themselves, and those who provide services. During our visit, we didn't encounter anything related to this debate. For that matter, we saw very few anglers.

John's raft had swivel seats fore and aft and where we launched, two anglers in a canoe and another in a pontoon boat put in right before us. Soon after getting underway, we passed the anglers in the canoe as they had stopped to wade fish. One was fighting a fish as we drifted by. Soon thereafter, Chris and I began to catch cutthroat with hopper patterns. The fishing wasn't fast, but to be able to catch fish as we drifted right through town was amazing. As we continued on our way, clouds began to build and we had some light showers. Since our drift was to cover only about five miles, we stopped periodically to fish by wading knowing we had plenty of time before reaching the take out. At 2:30, the overcast disappeared and sun came out to stay. When this happened, the fishing picked up considerably. We had a lunch of deli sandwiches after fishing a pool, within sight of town, from which we landed four cutthroat. While we ate, the anglers in the canoe drifted by and we saw no one fishing for the rest of our drift.

At 3:30, the fishing became as good as you could want. We pinched

About halfway on our drift with John Kendal through the town of Fernie down to Cokato, we stopped to have lunch. As we ate, a canoe with two anglers drifted by. They were the only two anglers we saw for the entire day.

tip line. To the ten-pound tippet, a #4 White Marabou Muddler was attached. You would think this mouthful of a fly would attract a larger predator, but nearly the opposite took place. The Muddler accounted for two fish, a seventeen-inch cutthroat and a fourteen-inch bull trout.

At 6:00, the sun dropped behind the hills and the air temperature plummeted. We were glad we had brought along jackets. John proved to be a very good guide, easy to get along with, pleasant in his ways with helping us and knowledgeable about the river. Not long after the drift was completed, rain started to fall and thunder began. It continued through much of the night. The weather was deteriorating and we hoped the worst of it would pass before morning arrived. We spent the night in Fernie at the Cedar Lodge Motel, where we also had a pleasant meal. There were many places offering accommodations in town and the newest was the Super 8. A listing of some of the businesses appears at the end of this report.

With puddles remaining from the rain during the night and a light rain falling, we drove to Elko to meet Kelly Laatsch the next morning. Our fishing gear was loaded into Kelly's Suburban and we drove to the Morrisey Access, about nine miles upstream. Like the day before under better weather, we began with hopper patterns and began to hook cutthroat right away. A mile into the drift, it began to rain. With the rain came wind and in spite of this the cutthroat continued to rise.

Kelly is an excellent guide and helped Chris with her mending techniques. He offered tips that improved my fishing too. Up until we stopped for lunch at around 2:00, we continued using hoppers with good results. To give us some relief from the rain while eating lunch, Kelly beached the boat on a bar under some trees along the bank. With portable chairs erected and using the ice chest as a table, he put out a spread of fried chicken, personally-made deer sausage, fresh rolls, chips, sliced cucumbers and chocolate chip cookies. While we ate, a hatch of large mayflies began. They were a size 12 and looked like some kind of Ephemerella, similar to the drakes that we see on the Upper Sacramento in California in mid June. Interrupting lunch, I showed a hopper to a couple of fish, which rose regularly along the bank close to the boat. They refused. Switching to a #12 Yellow Humpy, I was able to hook both cutthroats. Each was about the same size, about fifteen inches.

After lunch, we came to some slower water where Kelly said mayfly imitations would produce better than hoppers. My choice was a #14 Adams

Paradun and Chris chose a #12 Irresistible. Although the hatch was not intense, there was no doubt that the cutthroat were well aware of the presence of this mayfly and our flies were well received. When we came again to more broken water, hopper imitations were exchanged for the mayflies. I tied on a Dave's Hopper and Kelly tied on one of his parachute-hackled hopper patterns for Chris. For a while, Chris outfished me 5:1. It didn't take long for me to realize that a hopper pattern lying lower in the water like a natural was preferred to one that rode higher.

When we entered the canyon, the wind died to where it was almost pleasant. We enjoyed good fishing for forty-five minutes before a strong wind began to blow up the canyon. It blew so hard that Kelly had to work the oars with strong strokes to control the boat at times. We had hooked about thirty-five cutthroat by now and with the weather fast deteriorating, a run was made for the take-out during which time we fished infrequently. The take-out was reached at around 6:00.

This section that we drifted had a couple of places where trees had fallen into the water making boating hazardous. Kelly walked the boat around these obstacles as they could upset a boat. During our drift, we saw no other anglers. Chris and I had constant action, but to put things into perspective, Kelly mentioned that he guided a couple of experienced anglers a few days earlier under more pleasant weather. They landed over 100 cutthroat between them.

Elk River cutthroat typically measure between twelve and nineteen inches.

SUMMARY

Because of a two-year no-kill moratorium, which was partially lifted beginning with the 1998 season, the Elk River may be very close to carrying as many cutthroat as it has for many years. In the early season, fishing is done mostly with nymphs. Good dry-fly fishing doesn't take place until the waters become lower and clear. Our best guess is that fishing dries will be productive as early as mid July most years and early august following years of heavy winter precipitation.

Fishing pressure on the Elk has increased, but it isn't anything close to that found on the premium tailwater fisheries in the States. Should you come to fish the Elk, set aside enough time to sample other waters in the region. You might want to ask Kelly Laatsch and John Kendal about the fishing in the tributaries of the main streams. From what we understand, it may take a little more physical effort to reach these waters, but the rewards in the form of larger cutthroat may be waiting.

Businesses

The following are some of the businesses near Fernie, a town with a population of about 5,000 principally known for its ski slopes. Because it's a vacation destination, numerous B&Bs are available. For a more complete listing, contact the FERNIE CHAMBER OF COMMERCE and VISITOR INFOCENTRE, Highway #3 and Dicken Road, Fernie, BC, Canada V0B 1M0; Tel. 250-423-6868, FAX 250/423-3811, e-mail: fernie@elkvalley.net; website: www.city.fernie.bc.ca. All prices are given in Canadian dollars (unless noted) with exchange rates strongly favoring the U.S.

Accommodations

• CEDAR LODGE, 1101 7th Avenue, Fernie, BC, Canada V0B 1M0; Tel. 250-423-4622, 1-800-977-2977, FAX 250-423-3011, has rooms, a pool, whirlpool and sauna, lounge and restaurant. Rates for rooms start at around $50.

• SUPER 8 MOTEL, 2021 Highway #3, Fernie, BC, Canada V0B 1M0; Tel. l250-423-6788, FAX 250-423-6799, is the newest motel in Fernie. Rates for rooms begin at around $60. It is located on the west side of town close to a restaurant and gas station with convenience store.

• THREE SISTERS MOTEL, 441 Highway 3, Fernie, BC, Canada V0B 1M0. Tel. 250-423-4438, FAX 250-423-6220, has 36 units and is within walking distance of places to eat. Rates for rooms begin around $35, $10 additional for a kitchen.

• HI 3 LODGE, 891 Highway #3, Fernie, BC, Canada V0B 1M0. Tel. 800-667-1167, FAX 250-423-6004, has a coffee shop and some rooms with kitchen units. Room rates began at around $40 with kitchen units for $20 more.

RV Parks & Campgrounds

• MOUNT FERNIE PROVINCIAL PARK, KOOTENAY DISTRICT, Box 118, Wasa, BC, Canada V0B 2K0; Tel. 250-422-4200, has thirty-eight tent sights and is located about a mile west of Fernie. Sites are $9.50/night.

• SNOW VALLEY MOTEL & RV PARK, 1041 Highway #3, Box 1530, Fernie, BC, Canada V0B 1M0; Tel. 250-423-4421, has ten sites for RVs (no tent camping) with full hookup around $16/night.

• WEST CROW CAMPGROUND, Highway #3, Box 1000, Elko, BC, Canada V0B 1J0; Tel. 250-529-7445, offers full hookup for RVs, tent camping sites, laundry, store, showers and restaurant. Full hookups are $15/night and tent sites are $10/night.

Guides & Outfitters

Since fishing with John Kendal and Kelly Laatsch, Kelly has opened ST. MARY ANGLERS FLYSHOP, #1340 Mark Street, Kimberly, BC, Canada V1A 3A1; Tel. 800-667-2311, and website: stmaryangler.com. They provide guiding in streams and lakes in southeast British Columbia for flyfishers of all skill levels. We found Kelly Laatsch and John Kendal to be extremely competent and amiable. The guide rates were $325 U. S./day for two anglers in 2002. This included lunch and a couple of flies per angler. A charge of $1.50/fly was charged thereafter. To guarantee a date, booking two months in advance of a trip is suggested.

• KOOTENAY FLY SHOP & GUIDING CO., Gordon Silverthorne, Proprietor, 821 7th Avenue, Box 1883, Fernie, BC, Canada V0B 1M0; Phone/Fax 250-423-4483, e-mail: kootnfly@elkvalley.net and website: www.rockies.net/~kootnfly/ is a full-service fly shop renting canoes and rafts and provides shuttles.

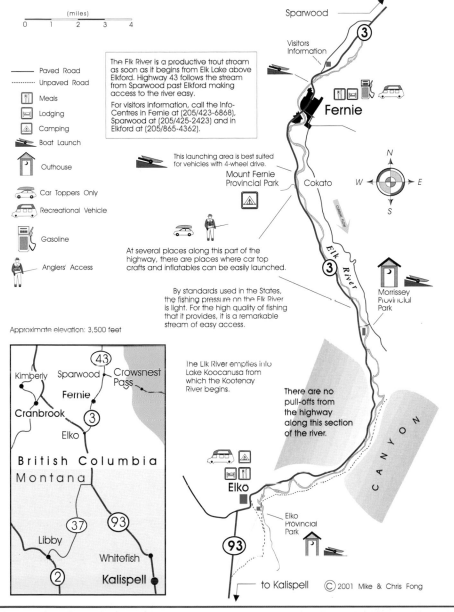

Sparwood

Visitors Information

The Elk River is a productive trout stream as soon as it begins from Elk Lake above Elkford. Highway 43 follows the stream from Sparwood past Elkford making access to the river easy.

For visitors information, call the Info-Centres in Fernie at (205/423-6868), Sparwood at (205/425-2423) and in Elkford at (205/865-4362).

Fernie

This launching area is best suited for vehicles with 4-wheel drive.

Mount Fernie Provincial Park

Cokato

At several places along this part of the highway, there are places where car top crafts and inflatables can be easily launched.

Morrissey Provincial Park

By standards used in the States, the fishing pressure on the Elk River is light. For the high quality of fishing that it provides, it is a remarkable stream of easy access.

The Elk River empties into Lake Koocanusa from which the Kootenay River begins.

There are no pull-offs from the highway along this section of the river.

CANYON

(miles)
0   1   2   3   4

— Paved Road
.... Unpaved Road
Meals
Lodging
Camping
Boat Launch
Outhouse
Car Toppers Only
Recreational Vehicle
Gasoline
Anglers' Access

Approximate elevation: 3,500 feet

Kimberly   Sparwood   (43)   Crowsnest Pass
Fernie
Cranbrook   (3)
Elko

British Columbia
Montana

(37)   (93)
Libby
Whitefish
(2)   Kalispell

Elko
Elko Provincial Park
(93)
to Kalispell   © 2001 Mike & Chris Fong

An Elk River cutthroat with the Muddler Minnow it struck.

ELK RIVER

GREEN RIVER

5 *Southwest Wyoming*

GREEN RIVER

*U*tah's Green River is most famous, among flyfishers, where it flows from Flaming Gorge Reservoir. Fish counts are some of the highest of any tailwater fishery in the West and the trout are not particularly difficult to catch. As a multiple-use river also popular with rafters, the number of people drifting on any given summer day can boggle the mind. Rangers keep an accurate record of river users and daily counts over 1,000 are normal. To avoid recreational drifters who far outnumber anglers, most flyfishers come to the stream in May and early June when the weather can be pleasant and before school lets out. It has been our experience that recreational drifters, comprised mainly of students who arrive by the busloads, don't represent much of a problem. They are usually content to have water fights, filling their buckets with water and flinging it at occupants of other boats. For the greatest majority of the time, their boats remain out of the main current where most of the fishing takes place. Still, the atmosphere that prevails on the river after mid June is not what most anglers want to confront. There are ways to avoid the crowds. You can start your drift early in the morning well before recreational drifting begins or you can fish the river below the first take-out at Little Hole. Recreational drifters rarely go beyond Little Hole. If they want to do more drifting, they usually make a second run starting again at the dam.

Chris and I have had excellent fishing on the Green below Flaming Gorge on our own and guided by Dennis Breer of Trout Creek Flies. We've had good fishing on the Green near Pinedale, Wyoming. In our opinion, some of the most interesting fishing on the Green takes place on the river flowing from Fontenelle Reservoir and through the Seedskadee National Wildlife Preserve. For thirty miles or more, the Green

The Green River flowing from Fontenelle Reservoir is a big, prairie river populated with cutthroat, rainbow and brown trout, some growing to good size.

Besides rainbows and brown trout, there are good-sized cutthroat in the river too.

winds its way through prairie land not yet discovered by the angling hoards. Even if it was "discovered," I'm not sure that a high percentage of anglers would return. There are not large concentrations of trout like below Flaming Gorge and there isn't the scenic beauty of the river by Pinedale where the Wind River Range forms an impressive backdrop. There are also mosquitoes and deer flies. What makes the Green such an attraction are good-size cutthroat, rainbow and brown that are challenging to catch. If you are an angler looking for less crowded, yet easily accessed water, one who gains satisfaction knowing you have caught trout that would elude the average angler, this part of the Green is what you're looking for. Our assessment of the stream has been echoed by a good number of our subscribers who have tasted what the Green below Fontenelle can produce. Most of these readers have landed trout weighing more than five pounds, some have hooked them near ten and there was one particular brown that was hooked and nearly landed that was a true leviathan. Considering that the huge trout of Flaming Gorge Reservoir migrate up this section of the Green to spawn and sometimes linger is fuel enough to trigger your imagination.

To experience the best of what this part of the Green has to offer, you will need the services of one of the best guides Chris and I have ever met. Bennie Johnson is that unique individual with infectious enthusiasm matched with experience and skill that makes any angler perform better than he or she normally does. On those rare days when he isn't guiding, he is on the river experimenting and exploring so his clients will always have the best chances to be successful. He delights in seeing his anglers catch fish, but more importantly, Bennie makes sure they have a good time. After fishing with him, you could fish on your own and do reasonably well, but I suspect that those who can afford his services would rather pay for the pleasure of his company. A more genuine and humble person would be difficult to find. If The Inside Angler posted a list of the best guides encountered in our travels, Bennie Johnson would be in the top tier not just for the service he provides, but as a shining example of what most of us want to find in a fellow human being.

GREEN RIVER

One of the graphics we use in The Inside Angler shows what anglers can expect to catch at each reported location. We try to take into account many factors and then display conservative figures. Many subscribers have reported catches far greater than what we consider optimum results. This possibility always exists when fishing under the best of conditions combined with a high skill level. If fishing results fall into the minimum category, it can probably be attributed to the presence of negative factors beyond anyone's control. We come face to face with poor conditions periodically and this was the case in 1996 on the Green River downstream of Fontenelle Reservoir in Wyoming. This section of the river is not to be confused with the Green flowing downstream of Flaming Gorge Reservoir, one the most prolific trout streams in the West. During the time of our visit, the winds were blowing so strong that our boat was actually being blown upstream against the current. Our guide had to hike back to the highway and hitch a ride to retrieve his rig. Luckily, the place where our drift ended was easily reached by a dirt road.

Chris and I returned in July 1997 to the Green River below Fontenelle Reservoir and experienced fishing at the opposite end of the scale from the year before. We had three days of near perfect weather, and I believe we were in the care of the best guide on this section of the Green River. We had heard from anglers, including some of our subscribers, that this section of the Green was worth fishing. We now know first-hand that it is. But there is some risk to fishing in regards to the weather, especially the wind. It can be dead calm one day and howling the next.

During the International Sportsmen's Exposition in San Mateo in 1997, Chris and I met Bennie Johnson of Highland Desert Flies, a guide service in Green River, Wyoming. He had a booth at the show with some photographs of impressive trout taken on the Green below Fontenelle. Bennie was confident he could show us good fishing without a lot of competition from other anglers. Chris and I arrived at the town of Green River late in the evening on Thursday, July 31. We spent the night in our van conversion at Tex's Travel Camp, an RV park at the west end of town. Bennie came by to visit after his guide trip that day. He said he would be back at 6:30 in the morning to pick us up. The Green River flowed right by the RV Park where we stayed. At dusk as we sat on the picnic bench at our site, we saw a few trout rise. The fish appeared small and we didn't fish.

When we awoke, skies were clear and it was calm. After Bennie arrived, it took a drive of about forty minutes to reach a place within the Seedskadee National Wildlife Area where we would begin our drift. Before Bennie left to do the shuttle, he said it might be worthwhile to fish. In the half hour before he returned, I landed a small brown and a large whitefish.

In this section, the Green is a large, prairie river too deep to wade across and measuring more than 200 feet wide in most places. The bottom land through which the river flows is wide and undisturbed with few trees along the banks. Antelope are frequently seen in the wildlife area,

as are moose. When not found by the river, moose favor the marshlands adjacent to the stream where there are numerous ponds. With the abundance of standing water, the results of a winter with far above normal precipitation, mosquitoes were thick. We found that whenever we were on the banks, these biting insects would quickly find us. Out on the river, they were hardly noticed.

As we began our drift at 8:00, swarms of Tricos filled the air. The most prominent insects on the water were midges. These were probably the reasons for the intermittent rises. To begin, Bennie suggested that we use a Royal Stimulator with either a scud imitation or a San Juan Worm for a dropper. These were tied onto a five-foot length of 4x leader secured to the hook bend of the large dry. My Stimulator accounted for a fourteen-inch rainbow right away. I next hooked a big cutthroat. After fighting the trout for several minutes, Bennie beached the boat so Chris could photograph its capture. It was a heavy cutthroat more than twenty inches long. Even so, its fight was far more than a fish like this could usually muster. As the cutthroat was drawn closer, we could see that the nymph was embedded in its right pectoral fin. Before we could net it, the hook pulled free.

We next landed a few small rainbows up to thirteen inches. While we fished, I noticed that Bennie was concentrating his attention on specific areas along the shore as if he was looking for something in particular. When we approached what appeared to be a man-made, submerged rock dam locals called a sill, Bennie oared the dory across the river below the structure. Just upstream along a steep cliff, a pod of fish was feeding on the surface. After resting the water to make sure they were not disturbed, Chris began making presentations. On her second cast, the stimulator was taken. It was one of those slow, confident rises often made by a good-size trout. After feeling the bite of the hook, it raced downstream a good distance and held its ground. I thought we might have to lift anchor to give chase, but after constant prodding it swam back upstream below the rock dam. After that it was only a matter of a couple of tense moments before the 23-inch rainbow was landed.

I was up next. After Chris' battle with the rainbow, the fish became suspicious and didn't begin feeding again for a few minutes. When they did, they wouldn't come all the way to the top. By watching closely, I could see the water bulge as they came close to the surface to take nymphs. Within a few casts with the Stimulator and dropper nymph combination, I had a fish take the

Rounding a bend in the river, we came upon a moose feeding in the shallows. When it saw us, it quickly retreated to shore and soon disappeared.

Unless fish are seen actively feeding on the surface to suggest the use of dry flies, we often fished a worm, nymph or scud imitation beneath a large attractor fly.

There were three trout feeding just below the surface at this break in the current and all of them looked to be sizable. Mike presents a nymph to the last one in line.

Pheasant Tail. This fish fought differently. It stayed down and was determined not to be lifted to the surface. Finally, it tired and Bennie netted a heavy, nineteen-inch cutthroat. After this, the remaining fish went down to stay.

Without any signs of fish feeding, Bennie said it was possible, at times, to get trout to strike the Stimulator or the Pheasant Tail Nymph if they were activated by retrieving them downstream. I was skeptical, but it only took several casts for Bennie to have a strike. We never saw the fish because when the rod was lifted to set the hook, the 4x tippet parted.

We next came to a scum hole, an eddy off the main current where foam and floating detritus blanketed the water and spun slowly in an elongated oval. Where the current passed by the debris, a couple of fish rose. Giving the trout wide berth, Bennie quietly oared up behind them and beached the boat. He said it would be best to make our approach from the grass bank that lay opposite the fish. On hands and knees, we moved forward slowly. In order to have a chance with both trout, I tried first for the one downstream. Placing the flies just upstream of where I saw the fish last, I watched for any kind of sign that would suggest a take. For an instant, the Stimulator hesitated in its drift and I raised the rod. The trout had taken the scud. It was sizable and shot downstream and out toward the middle of the river. Bennie said there weren't any underwater obstacles so I worked the fish downstream so the other trout would not be disturbed. It was a long and determined fight, but soon Bennie netted a twenty-one-inch rainbow.

The other trout was also a rainbow. We could see its back every now and then

when it rose. Bennie said it might be as large as twenty-six or twenty-seven inches. It was Chris' turn. The rainbow was not holding position and moved upstream and down in a narrow band of water next to the scum as it fed. With coaching from Bennie, the rainbow finally took the scud as signaled by the movement of the Stimulator. For an instant, there was tension on Chris' line, but the hook only pricked the jaw of the big rainbow. The line went slack.

It was now clear to me that Bennie liked to fish for trout in the same manner as I did. He'd look for the largest fish and then try to get us into position to convert the opportunity. By his own admission, Bennie was a hog hunter. There are anglers not of this thinking who tell of satisfaction with smaller rewards, but this approach does not motivate me to perform at my best. I feel more comfortable with Bennie's approach.

We next came to a flat studded with large boulders, some protruding above the surface. There were as many as ten or twelve trout rising simultaneously in a 100-yard stretch. I landed a sixteen-inch brown on the Stimulator and then asked to be dropped on the shore so Chris and I could both fish at the same time. Downstream at a bend where the boulders were no more, there were several trout rising near the bank in shallow water. One seemed large and I concentrated my efforts on it. After a few casts, it quit feeding. I switched to a #14 Black Foam Beetle. It accounted for a small brown that I failed to hook. By this time, Chris and Bennie drifted down to where I was and we continued downstream.

Chris and Bennie show the rainbow before it is released.

For awhile, we fished from the boat. Bennie moved us into position so we could cast to side riffles, breaks along the cliffs where rocks fallen from the face created holding areas on the downstream side and to large submerged boulders. Chris and I had some takes from good-size trout but failed to hook any of them solidly. We then came to a place that Bennie called the Hog Hole. At the bottom of this deep pool, the water flowed back upstream in a big, slow backwash. A big brown took my scud dropper. The fish was plainly seen in shallow water before it dove for the bottom. It was on for a couple of minutes and then the hook pulled free. Our bad luck continued at the head of the pool where the eddy met the main current. A sizable cutthroat took a Stimulator, but it was not hooked solidly either.

Next we came to a pool Bennie said was best fished by wading and presenting a nymph with an indicator. Chris doesn't particularly like to fish in this manner and I tried it for a while without any strikes. The current split at the head with the main flow running down the far side along some rocks placed there to protect the bank. A bar in midstream allowed wading close to make presentations. As Chris and I watched with cameras ready, Bennie used a San Juan Worm with a couple of shots to take it to the bottom. He first foul-hooked a twenty-inch rainbow at the top of the pool and then landed a beautiful rainbow that measured twenty-five inches. This fish was holding at the spot where both currents came together before flowing around a sweeping bend.

Bennie's rainbow was the last good fish that was taken on this day. For the rest of the afternoon until dusk, we saw very few fish rise. This was surprising because there was no wind and large swarms of mating caddis promised something better. At a spot just upstream from the take-out, we spent fifteen minutes on some very difficult fish that were rising to something other than caddis. By the time Bennie dropped us off at the RV Park back at Green River, it was 10:00. It had been a long day on the river. The only angler we saw was shore bound and an acquaintance of Bennie's. After eating and showering, it was after midnight before we went to sleep.

The next day was Saturday. Like the morning before, the skies were clear and it was calm. At our put-in, there was a boat with a guide and his companion. These anglers were from Park City, Utah on a busman's holiday. We shoved off at 8:45 and the other boat quickly passed us. There were plenty of Tricos on the water, but most of the insects were still airborne. Unlike the day before, there were fewer fish rising. I tied on a Mercer

Stone Fly nymph as a dropper from the Royal Stimulator and had a strike on my second cast. It was a sixteen-inch cutthroat. As we drifted looking for working fish, a breeze began to blow.

The larger fish that we were finding the day before were not moved to feed on this morning. There were rises, but mainly made by small fish. At one run, which I fished by wading, I landed five trout. All were cutthroat except for one rainbow. The largest might have measured eleven inches. Bennie had taken Chris downstream and when I caught up with them, they reported encountering only small trout too. With nothing much going on, we stopped for lunch.

After eating, the fishing perked up a bit. Along a cliff, where piles of rocks formed little breaks in the current, we found some larger fish. The first was an eighteen-inch rainbow. It took a scud dropper. Fifty yards downstream from where this rainbow was landed, we found several trout rising simultaneously. Chris and I both cast to these fish and I was the first to hook up. The trout shot off downstream taking me into my backing as only a big rainbow could. Bennie dug the oars in deep and we finally caught up with the trout far down on the opposite side of the river. I disembarked to finish the battle and Bennie followed with his net. To our surprise, the rainbow took off again acting every bit like the battle had just begun. Bennie ran back to get the boat because it might be needed again. When he returned, the rainbow was worked in close enough to net. It only measured twenty-one inches, a sprinter with enough staying power to be a long-distance racer.

At a run opposite a wing dam leading into a sweeping pool, a trout made a huge boil after taking Chris's San Juan Worm dropper. It swam downstream with the kind of power that could only come from beats of a broad tail. Then the trout reversed its course and turned back upstream into the strong current. It headed for some

At the sight of the net, Chris' rainbow made a last attempt to break free.

The rainbow that was feeding above this one was considerably larger, but it quit feeding after this one was landed.

SUMMARY

The best of the fishing lasts from July through October. If you can endure the cold, good fishing with streamers continues into November. For the waters within the Seedskadee Wildlife Refuge, only four outfitter permits are issued. Bennie Johnson of Highland Desert Flies holds one of these permits and is acknowledged as the most proficient guide on the river. He is tireless with a good sense of humor. If you are not comfortable fishing from early morning to dusk, be sure to make him aware of this. He'll fish you until you say quit. He may appear to be a little rough around the edges, but Bennie aims to please. A big plus when fishing with Bennie is that he provides all flies as part of the fee. He is in the process of training some guides to work with him. If you prefer to fish on your own, the river is rated Class I for drifting. We encountered no rapids, but anglers unfamiliar with the river should make inquiries before launching to make a drift.

The cost of Wyoming Fishing Licenses for non-residents are $5/one-day, $20/five days or $30/ten days. A season Nonresident Fishing License is $50. The Green River from Sweetwater County Road 8 (4.5 miles below Fontenelle Dam) to the confluence of Big Sandy River is restricted to the use of artificial flies or lures only. The limit is one-trout per day, which must measure more than twenty inches.

Our fishing was done with #4-weight and #5-weight systems matched to double-taper and weight-forward floating lines. The fish did not appear leader shy and we used 12 to 14 foot. leaders tapered to 4x and 5x tippets. We did not fish streamers, which might call for sinking-tip or full sinking-lines.

submerged limbs at the head of the run unseen by us. There was nothing Chris could do but to follow and watch. When the trout no longer moved, Bennie waded across the heavy flow with the line running through a ring made by a thumb and forefinger. He couldn't free the line and returned to get Chris's rod. Upon reaching the opposite bank, he was able to work the line free. Winding the line back onto the reel as he headed upstream, he soon saw a brown. It was finning quietly in three feet of water with the leader wrapped around a stout limb. As Bennie dipped the tip end of the rod into the water to try to free the line, the brown made a surge and the tippet parted. Bennie said the brown was in the thirty-inch class. This got him very excited.

For the remainder of the day, we hooked a few more trout, but none measured more than eighteen inches. The wind grew in intensity as dusk came upon us and we were glad to reach the take-out. We spent the night at Sweet Dreams Inn, the newest motel in Green River.

On Sunday, competition with other anglers for the water was much greater than our first two days. Chris and I fished separately. Bennie and I were in one boat and she was with Dennis Watts, one of Bennie's guides, in another. In addition to our boats, there were two other dories plus a rubber raft with three anglers. The fishing for us on this day was less productive than the previous days. A twenty-four-inch rainbow taken on a Royal Stimulator was the largest trout we landed. We landed three other trout eighteen inches or larger plus some smaller fish, but the fish were not active. Perhaps the gradual lowering of the flow starting on Saturday from 1,100 cfs to a projected low of 750 cfs within a couple of weeks was responsible for the down turn in our fishing. This reduction of the water was necessary to work on some of the sills. My impression of the fishing on this stretch of the Green is that if you seek larger-than-average trout that are challenging to catch without a lot of competition from other anglers, you will find it here. On the day of our departure, a storm moved in with high winds and rain.

What Guide Bennie Johnson likes to do is to drift along looking for feeding fish. When big fish are spotted, he likes his anglers to disembark from the boat and make presentations on foot.

Businesses

Restaurants and accommodations can be found in the towns of La Barge on Highway 189 north of Fontenelle Reservoir, the town of Green River off Interstate 80 and at Rock Springs, which is located about twelve miles east of Green River. Rock Springs is the largest city in Sweetwater County and has a commercial airport. Below are listed some of the businesses close to the fishing with which we had first-hand experience. For a more complete list of services free upon request, contact the GREEN RIVER CHAMBER OF COMMERCE, 1450 Unita Drive, Green River, WY 82935; Tel. 307-875-5711 and ROCK SPRINGS CHAMBER OF COMMERCE, 1987 Dewar Drive, Rock Springs, WY 82901; Tel. 307-362-3771. Campgrounds are located below Fontenelle Dam and at Slate Creek, which is about four and one half miles downstream. Bring your own drinking water.

• HIGHLAND DESERT FLIES, BENNIE AND CONNIE JOHNSON, 1700 Wilson #39, Green River, WY 82935, Tel. 307-875-2358, is the most qualified guide service in the area. Bennie is an excellent fly tier and creates flies especially for this particular section of the Green River. Guide rates are $350/day, and include lunch, beverages and flies.

To be successful, anglers must be able to cast with a high degree of accuracy, sometimes in windy conditions. This fishing is not for beginners. Reservations in advance are strongly suggested, particularly if you want to fish with Bennie. A shuttle from the airport in Rock Springs can be arranged for $25.

• SWEET DREAMS INN, 1410 Unita, Green River, WY 82935; Tel. 307-875-7554, is the newest motel in town. Rates for a double were about $60/night.

• SUPER 8 MOTEL, 280 West Flaming Gorge, Green River, WY 82935; Tel. 800-800-8000, is an older facility, but clean. Rates begin at around $40/single and $48/double.

• TEX'S TRAVEL CAMP, Star Route 2, Box 101, Green River, WY 82935; Tel. 307-875-2630, is located at the west side of Green River next to the river. There are many pull-throughs for large RVs plus sites exclusively set aside for tent camping. We found the showers clean and the grounds well maintained. Some sites include cable TV connections. Rates are moderate.

• EMBERS RESTAURANT, 95 East Railroad Avenue, Green River, WY 82935; Tel. 307-875-9983, is popular with locals and serves good food with friendly service. It is open seven days a week for breakfast, lunch and dinner. Prices are moderate.

• CRUEL JACK'S, at the junction of Interstate 80 and U.S. Highway 191 (Exit 307), is a truck stop with a popular restaurant. The menu is typical American, the service friendly and the prices are moderate.

• FONTENELLE SERVICE, Michael Marble, proprietor, Star Route 1, Kemmerer, WY 83101; Tel. 307-877-4844, is located on Highway 372 about five miles below Fontenelle Reservoir. It has groceries, gas and does shuttles. The cost for the average shuttle is around $15-50. Michael is also a licensed guide.

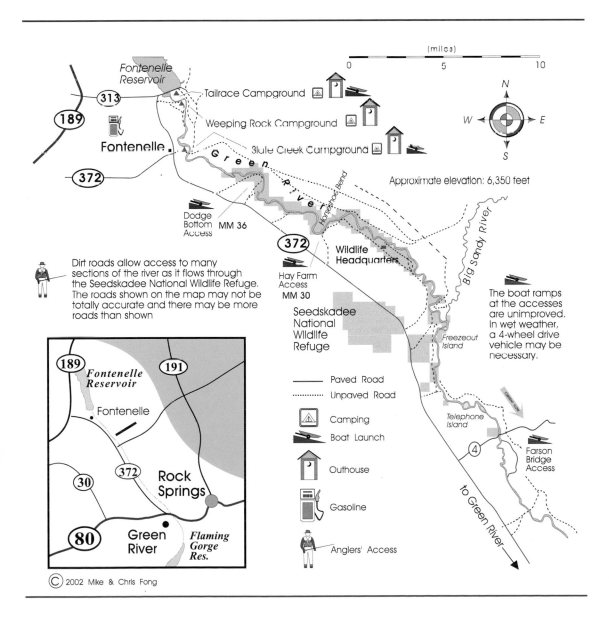

Dirt roads allow access to many sections of the river as it flows through the Seedskadee National Wildlife Refuge. The roads shown on the map may not be totally accurate and there may be more roads than shown

The boat ramps at the accesses are unimproved. In wet weather, a 4-wheel drive vehicle may be necessary.

Paved Road
Unpaved Road
Camping
Boat Launch
Outhouse
Gasoline
Anglers' Access

Approximate elevation: 6,350 feet

© 2002 Mike & Chris Fong

GREEN RIVER

LOWER SACRAMENTO RIVER

6 North Central California

LOWER SACRAMENTO RIVER

When Chris and I started fishing the lower Sacramento River fifteen years ago, we were immediately impressed with the fish. They were good size and they were wild. Their sharp fins and hard bodies exhibited all the best qualities of trout born in a stream. With the help of local anglers Brad Jackson, Jim Murphy, Ernie Denison and Mike Mercer, who we fished with at different times, we were introduced to methods that we could employ to catch fish consistently. For the most part, these approaches always made the assumption that the rainbows would be feeding near or on the bottom. Fishing with dry flies, except for a very short period at dusk, was not productive. Chris and I would rather fish with dry flies, but we'll fish whatever method is required to catch wild trout, particularly if the fish are as wonderful as those found on the lower Sacramento.

There are many possible reasons why trout refuse to rise, even when there are many flies floating on the surface. One reason can be that there are so many organisms near the bottom that it isn't necessary for trout to rise in the water column to find food. This must be the case for the rainbows of the lower Sacramento River near Redding because the substrata are awash with organisms. Not only do the trout rarely leave the bottom to feed, but once a trout chooses a feeding lane, it doesn't move much laterally to chase items to eat. This explains why a run must be fished thoroughly in order to be successful. Every foot should be covered, and the offering must drift through drag free. On this stream, more than any other, we see anglers employing the "stack" mend. This is a technique where excess line is thrown on the water upstream from where the nymph lands and starts its drift downstream. A stack mend is done with a move that can be described as a half hearted roll cast. Refined, it

A popular place to fish is right in the town of Redding at an area known as the Posse Grounds. There is a picnic area here, as well as a boat launch.

can look like a twist of the wrist to roll the tip of the rod over abruptly, which will cause a loop of line to roll toward the line already on the water. If the stroke to achieve the mend is too strong, like actually making a roll cast, the settling nymph will be disturbed. Done correctly and in moderation, this extra line stacked behind the fly removes any chance for the nymph to be affected by conflicting currents. As the nymph continues drifting, mends are thrown in as needed. Stack mending with an indicator and a short line nymphing method are probably the most useful techniques practiced on the river. Throwing a stack mend takes some practice, but is well worth the investment of time to learn. It is easier to accomplish with a fast action rod than one that is slow. A double taper line or a Scientific Anglers Steelhead taper works better than a weight forward line because the bellies of these lines are of longer length and react more favorably to this technique.

Even under its lowest flows, the Sacramento by Redding is a big river. To cover the water, we've drifted the stream in our prams and in our canoe. At times, our canoe was used only to gain access to a part of the stream not fished frequently by others. One place we liked to fish was the inside of the bend upstream from the

Deschutes Bridge. We'd launch our canoe off the bridge embankment on the opposite side of the river, paddle across and then spend a couple of hours or more fishing before paddling back. Access to the river can be gained by foot in several places for those who don't use a boat. The Rodeo Grounds is a popular foot access, as is Turtle Bay Regional Park. At the Bonnyview Access, there are several good runs on the inside of an island. Cascade Community Park off Girvan Road is another access by an island. If the releases from the dam get too low, the channel will not hold as many trout and most of the rises you'll see are made by rough fish. Under lower flows, you'll want to hike across the island to the main flow.

Most streams have up and down cycles when fish populations can fluctuate. Since 1996, the Sacramento River by Redding has been on a high. One thing that may have helped the trout become more robust has been a new flow regimen where the water temperature is controlled to be much cooler and more comfortable during the summer. According to biologists, this has made the trout feed more voraciously than when the water was warmer and as a result, the trout are in much better shape. Guides familiar with the stream say the average trout has increased in size

The lower Sacramento River by Redding is a big river with flows that reach more than 15,000 cubic feet per second during the height of the irrigation season. The most popular times to fish the river are in the spring and autumn when flows are reduced. With no rapids to speak of, the river can be drifted with a variety of crafts.

and some even say the Sacramento by Redding may be the best trout stream in the West. This may be pushing the issue, but statistical data showing the presence of healthier and larger fish than before when there was a negative thermal influence cannot be disputed.

The Sacramento River is part of a water transport system and flows are often governed by agricultural needs, especially during the warmer months. During the summer, as much as 15,000 cfs of water is released from Keswick Dam. You would think that such an amount of water would make flyfishing futile, but it doesn't. As an example, Chris and I were visiting with Mike and Bertha Michalak of The Fly Shop at their home along the river not long ago in August. As evening approached, Mike and I took a ride in his jet-driven boat upstream to where the stream made a wide sweeping bend. In the twilight, trout began to feed on the surface on emerging caddis. Some of the trout were sizable and perhaps one was the seven and one half pound rainbow Mike had caught on a dry fly and released two weeks earlier. We didn't have our rods with us as darkness was fast approaching, but I wish we had.

After the height of summer flows, releases are reduced as irrigation needs are no longer required. By mid October, the releases can be down to 7,000 cfs. Some of the best fishing of the year takes place after the first dramatic draw down, but it doesn't happen immediately. It takes a few days to a week before the trout adjust to the lower flows. Catches by guided anglers after the river flows are stabilized range from a dozen to as many as thirty fish per day for two clients. Most anglers believe that wade fishing becomes feasible when flows drop to approximately 6,000 cfs. It is important to remember that even at these releases, the Sacramento is still a very large river with a powerful current. For myself, I am much more comfortable with flows less than 6,000 cfs. The early autumn fishing is done primarily with caddis pupa imitations, some with bead heads. Beginning in late October, salmon begin to spawn and there is a decided advantage in using a single egg pattern. If the winter is mild and rain isn't so heavy that the water becomes discolored, I like to look for rising fish that are taking Baetis off the surface. A couple of winters ago, Chris and I fished with guide Ernie Denison. Although most of the fish we caught were on nymphs, I did find some fish near the tail of a long, slow pool that were rising. The largest proved to be a rainbow around 18 inches. To find rising fish in the winter is not common, but it isn't that unusual either. These rising fish always seem to prefer the mid

part or the tail of long pools and the day must be calm. With a few exceptions, I don't expect to see a lot of fish rising at the same time. However, the rainbows are always decent size.

At times, the winter Baetis hatch can be intense. On a visit to the stream when we were shooting a segment for an outdoors TV show, we encountered such an emergence. The day was gray and cloudy and there was no wind, exactly the kind of weather conducive to Baetis hatches. We were fishing at the tail of a long pool where most of the water was forced to go around an island while the remainder flowed through a sweeping channel. The Baetis covered the water in this secondary flow, but we never saw a rise. Using a short line nymphing method to present a #16 dark mayfly nymph, which I probed the bottom with the aid of a split shot, I was able to catch a beautiful 19-inch male with a developing hook jaw for the camera.

One of the best times to be fishing on the stream is in the weeks leading up to the intense caddis hatches in early spring. In most years, the start of this massive emergence occurs around March 1. Once the hatch begins, trout feed heavily because the warming water increases their metabolism and the countless caddis pupa wiggling out of their cases are easy prey. Once satiated, it seems as though the rainbows must

Homes are located along parts of the river. This black lab belonging to one of the homeowners came out to join Mike as he fished.

The author gets ready to hand-land a rainbow.

digest their intake before feeding heavily again. This is the reason I believe that there may be lulls in the fishing whereas before the caddis appear; the trout feed constantly. A few years ago, we spent several days on the stream well after the emergence had begun.

In mid March, we fished with guide Barry Foster from The Fly Shop. He had invited us to fish with him a year earlier, but we never could coordinate a meeting. When we found the time, the river was not in the best of shape. There had been some heavy rain prior to our visit and the visibility was about 18 inches. I was very skeptical about our chances. At this time, Barry was having his anglers fish beads. As an old steelheader familiar with conventional gear, I knew exactly what he meant when he said that we'd be using the little plastic spheres with a hole drilled through the middle. This might be beyond the limits of what constitutes a fly, but I was curious. If we were against using beads, Barry said we could

The author nets a rainbow that took a deep drifted nymph. With so much food available to the trout at the bottom of the stream, it seems the rainbows don't have to overexert themselves to feed. For anglers to be successful, it is best to fish holding water very thoroughly, making many casts so all the feeding lanes are covered before moving to new water.

The lower Sacramento is not known as a stream that offers good dry-fly fishing. However, during the winter when small Baetis mayflies emerge in good numbers, it isn't unusual to find fish feeding on top in the tailouts of some of the slower-moving pools.

use any type of egg pattern we wanted. The salmon egg colored bead about a quarter of an inch in diameter was rigged by running the 3x tippet twice through the hole and then tying a #8 hook so it would dangle two inches from the bead. I asked Barry why he chose to rig this way. He said fish were always hooked in the jaw and never hooked so deep that they couldn't be released unharmed. To complete the rig, an indicator was placed nine feet above the bead and two bb size shots were placed a foot above the sphere.

We launched at the Rodeo Grounds at mid morning under clear skies and a little breeze. With a 10hp motor mounted on the transom of his drift boat, Barry first took us upstream to the riffles beneath the Highway 299 Bridge. Fishing from the boat, I had a take right away and turned over a nice fish, but failed to hook it. About five minutes later, I landed a beautiful rainbow around 20 inches long. For the rest of the day, until we pulled off the river at the Bonnyview access, we landed eight more rainbows and lost several others. On the day before, his anglers did twice that number. With the exception of a 14 incher, all the rainbows measured between 17 and 21 inches. Some of them fought so hard that Chris and I initially thought they were foul hooked. On the drift we encountered massive hatches of caddis, but saw only a few fish rise. Barry proved to be a very capable guide. He offered suggestions on how to improve our chances and had an easy-going manner.

On this same trip, we fished again with Ernie Denison. Our fishing results with Ernie were about the same as they were with Barry. The water clarity was worse than it was two days earlier with

only a foot of visibility. We put in at Bonnyview and took out at the Sacramento RV Park. Fish were caught on Copper Micro Z-Wing, Ernie's 2-Tone nymph, Glo Bugs and one was caught on a bead. We used #5 weight rods, nine feet long with floating lines. The air temperature rose to a warm 82 degrees.

In the summer of 1999, after the river rose to irrigation levels, some anglers experienced exceptional fishing. It was unexpected. Rainbows were caught mainly by swinging flies, not the usual nymph fishing with indicators. This was a dimension of the Sacramento River by Redding that was unfamiliar to most anglers, including myself.

The author nets a rainbow fooled by a small Adams.

SUMMARY

During winters of moderate rains, when the water levels of Shasta Lake are not allowed to become too high causing releases to be increased, fishing can be good during the coldest months of the year. Most anglers familiar with the river expect the best fishing to take place in the autumn after high irrigation flows are reduced and then again in the early spring at around the time of the famous caddis hatch.

Fishing is primarily done with nymphs, but single egg imitations can be used effectively from autumn—when salmon spawn—through the famous caddis hatch of spring. If you are not experienced with handling a boat in a river, the best option is to fish with a guide so the more productive places can be reached. In more moderate flows, personal float boats designed for moving water, prams, and canoes can be used to drift from access to access. There are no dangerous rapids, but the river flows swiftly even during lower flows. Two places where drifters should take extra precaution are where the stream takes a wide sweeper to the right downstream of the Bonnyview access and where the stream runs against the east bank below the Anderson Park launch. At the former, the river becomes compressed and gathers swift momentum as it passes through a chute. Preparations far in advance are needed for safe passage. You may want to stay to the left and walk your craft below the problem area before getting back on board. For the latter, you will want to stay to the inside of the bend. On the east side of the river where there are homes on the bluff, a series of cascades can upset a boat. There may be more places that are dangerous so it is important to ask personnel at The Fly Shop about these before doing a drift. The accompanying map shows some of the places where foot access is possible. When we fish on our own, we often use our canoe to get to the opposite side of the stream that is less fished.

Businesses

The following businesses in the area are some of the ones with which we've had personal contact. For a map of Redding, information packet, dining and hotel guide, contact the REDDING CONVENTION AND VISITORS BUREAU, 777 Auditorium Drive, Redding, CA 96001; Tel. 530-225-4100, 800-874-7562, FAX 530-225-4354

Motels

• BEST WESTERN PONDEROSA INN, 2220 Pine Street, Redding, CA 96001; Tel. 530-241-6300, has rates starting around $50/night.

• HOWARD JOHNSON, 2731 Bechelli Lane, Redding, CA 96002; Tel. 530-223-1935, has rates starting around $45/single and $50/double.

• SUPER 8 MOTEL, 5175 Churn Creek Road, Redding, CA 96002; Tel. 530-221-8881, is conveniently located at the Bonnyview off ramp near The Fly Shop. Rates were around $45/night/double.

Places to Eat

• GUIDO'S ITALIAN RESTAURANT, 1790 Market Street in Redding serves interesting food. We had a good meal there. It is one of the better restaurants in the area; Tel. 530-246-3922

• HATCH COVER RESTAURANT, 202 Hemsted Drive, Redding, CA 96001; Tel. 530-223-5606, is located high on the east bank of the river north of Cypress Avenue. It serves dinner daily with a menu that features preparations of beef, including Prime Rib, pastas, chicken and seafood. Prices are mostly moderate, but shellfish and large cuts of beef cost around $20. All entrees are served with soup, salad, sour dough bread served hot, and rice or potatoes.

• BIG RED'S BARBECUE, 2550 Bechelli Lane, Redding, CA 96001; Tel. 530-221-7427, specializes in take-out barbecue. A variety of meats and chicken are barbecued, and when we're lazy and staying in our RV, we often pick up an order of their pork ribs.

RV Parks

• THE SACRAMENTO RIVER RV PARK, 6596 Riverland Drive, Redding, CA 96002; Tel. 530-365-6402, FAX 530-365-2601, is located on the river south of Redding. Full hookups are around $20/night, which includes cable with thirty-three channels. A special area is set aside for tent camping, but it is closed after Labor Day.

• MARINA RV PARK, 2615 Park Marina Drive, Redding, CA 96001; Tel. 530-241-4396, is located in town just north of Cypress Street on the west side of the river. Fishing is possible within walking distance or by launching a small boat off the property. Full hookups were around $19/night. We found the showers clean and there is a convenience shop on the premises.

Guides

There are many capable guides working on the Sacramento River. The ones with whom we have fished and recommend are:

• ERNIE DENISON AND BARRY FOSTER, are experienced guides working out of The Fly Shop (see above). Besides guiding on the Sacramento River, Ernie also guides on other streams in northern California, including the Trinity River for steelhead.

• MIKE COSTELLO, PACIFIC ADVENTURES, 18582 Olive Street, Woodbridge, CA 95258; Tel. 209-367-5997, e-mail: fish-trips@fishtrips.net and website: fishtrips.net, guides for a variety of species on many waters in northern California. He guides anglers locally on the Sacramento/San Joaquin Delta for striped bass. Rates are around $275/day/two anglers, but vary depending on location and manner of fishing.

• DAVE SIMMONS, DAVE SIMMONS FLY FISHING ADVENTURES, 26152 Walch Avenue, Orland, CA 95963; Tel. 530-865-9630, guides for a variety of species in Northern California. He uses a jet-driven boat as well as a drift boat. His rates are $350/day for one or two anglers. Website: www.davesfishingadventures.com

Fly Shops

• THE FLY SHOP, MIKE AND BERTHA MICHALAK, proprietors, 4140 Churn Creek Road, Redding, CA 96002. Tel. 800-669-FISH, FAX 530-225-3555, e-mail: mike@theflyshop.com, and web site: www.theflyshop.com, is a full-service fly shop, well equipped, and has house guides. Guiding fees were $295/day for two anglers on the Sacramento River as of 2002. This included lunch, but did not include flies. Flies can be purchased at The Fly Shop, where guides meet with clients in the morning.

#20 Sawyer Pheasant Tail Nymph is a productive fly to use in the winter when Baetis may flies are active.

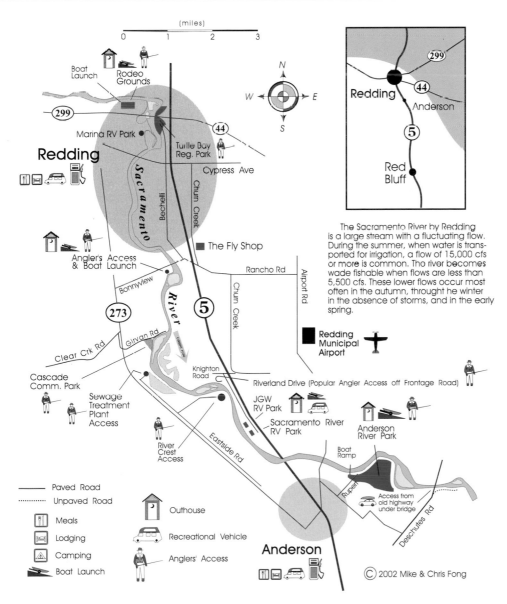

The Sacramento River by Redding is a large stream with a fluctuating flow. During the summer, when water is transported for irrigation, a flow of 15,000 cfs or more is common. The river becomes wade fishable when flows are less than 5,500 cfs. These lower flows occur most often in the autumn, throught he winter in the absence of storms, and in the early spring.

© 2002 Mike & Chris Fong

LOWER WILLIAMSON RIVER

7 South Central
Oregon

LOWER WILLIAMSON RIVER

*T*he lower Williamson River in south central Oregon is one of the finest wild trout streams in North America, particularly if you seek rainbows that approach the size of steelhead. It begins in the Yamsey Mountain area from a spring pond on Yamsi Ranch, which caters to flyfishers who catch-and-release some of the largest stream-dwelling brook trout in the West along with rainbows that can reach ten pounds. After flowing north through more ranch properties, the Williamson empties into Klamath Marsh, where there are few trout. The marsh divides the upper Williamson River from the lower with such a definitive boundary that fish populations are completely different in their respective waters. From the marsh, the Williamson continues north for a bit, swings to the west, and then heads south through a canyon to be joined by Spring Creek, which contributes greatly to its volume. Below the town of Chiloquin it is joined by the Sprague River before finally emptying into Klamath Lake. The Williamson River can offer excellent fishing from the opening of the season on the Saturday nearest Memorial Day, providing run-off from snow melt has been completed, to the end of the season on October 31. This review covers the river from the vicinity above Spring Creek downstream.

In past years, more and more restrictive angling regulations have been placed on the Williamson to preserve the indigenous rainbows. From the mouth to the Modoc Point Road Bridge, the limit is one trout a day. From here upstream to the bridge at Chiloquin, the limit is one trout between the Opening Day through July 31, and catch-and-release thereafter. No bait may be used as fishing is restricted to the use of artificial lures and flies. If fishing from a motorboat, the motor must not be running while fishing. From the Chiloquin Bridge to Kirk Bridge, one trout may be kept from Opening Day to July 31, and then it is catch-and-release the remainder of the season. Fishing is restricted to the use of artificial lures and flies from August 1 to October 31. Fishing is

An autumn sunset on the Williamson River.

Fishing at the confluence of Spring Creek, Chris brings a rainbow to net.

not allowed from any floating device that can support an angler.

One of my favorite times to fish the Williamson is during the last month and a half of the season. Gone are the mosquitoes of summer, which in some years are a terrible nuisance. Also gone are the crowds. Angling pressure is very light and the fishing gets better and better as the season draws to a close.

Each year the fishing on the Williamson River can be dramatically different. The reason for this is that many of the rainbows spend a considerable amount of time in Klamath Lake and their migrations into the stream never seem the same from year to year. Much of Klamath Lake is shallow and this may explain why some fish are always found in the river. In the early season, many fish, which have spawned, have not yet returned to the lake. During the heat of summer, the cooler waters of the river entice the rainbows out of the lake and the section from the Highway 97 Bridge to Chiloquin can be extremely productive. In the autumn, schools of fish migrate to the reaches of the river around Spring Creek with those already in the stream joining those ascending from the lake. These fall-run rainbows are in their prime and are considerably more robust than at any other time of year.

There is one very important key to fishing the Williamson River in the fall. To experience the best the stream has to offer, you must meet a major migration of fish. While there may be additional indicators, the one that I have found most reliable, for 35 years, is air temperature. As close as I can pin it down, it takes between ten days to two weeks for a significant migration of fish to reach the mouth of Spring Creek after the first freeze. If the air temperature hovers near freezing by the first of September, there will be a concentration of fish staging in the Chiloquin area by Labor Day. Most years, this scenario holds true to form and Chris and I have had some of the best autumn rainbow trout fishing that we have ever experienced at this time.

In years when it doesn't freeze until well into October, the major migrations of rainbows don't arrive in the vicinity of Spring Creek until the season closes. As recent as the autumn of 1998, it didn't freeze in southern Oregon until late October. Chris and I came to see what fish had migrated. We found some small schools of fish, but nothing compared to the numbers of fish that would arrive after the season's close.

If the desired weather pattern prevails, you can expect to find many rainbows at the Anglers' Access downstream from Chiloquin in early

The Williamson River upstream of the confluence of Spring Creek is not a large stream in the autumn. Migrating rainbows from lower down in the river often congregate in these waters.

September. The access is well marked, easy to find, and located about 300 yards from the highway junction on the road leading to town. It won't be hard to distinguish the migration because rainbows will be evident to the eye. All you have to do is stand on the levee and look into the water with polarized glasses during midday. It will be a remarkable sight. Best of all, though, these fish are vulnerable.

The best time to fish is under cloudy skies. If inclement weather prevails, by all means, try to fish until the front arrives. These are optimum conditions. My choice of fly would be a small, dark leech tied on a #10, 3x long hook. Before tying on three successive bunches of Marabou atop the hook, I weight the hook with ten wraps of medium lead wire. A weight forward floating line will work, as will a sink-tip, but a slow-sinking shooting taper will allow you to cover more water.

Private property exists from the boundary of the Anglers' Access upstream on the north bank. You cannot trespass. To legally fish upstream, you can use a boat or canoe to bypass the deep water, thereby transporting yourself to safe wading areas. By so doing, you will see giant, sunken logs and lava ledges that drop off into deep water. Fish

often hold near current breaks made by jutting lava ledges. Cast across and downstream, positioning your line so the fly sweeps near the current breaks. Most of the strikes will come on the drift or on the swing, but some will occur on the retrieve. I suggest an eight-pound test tippet at the end of a 12-foot leader. Use a heavier tippet in low-light conditions. It is legal to fish from a boat since this is below the Chiloquin Bridge provided you don't troll. If you don't feel comfortable wading, fishing from a boat might be best for you.

Anglers without a boat who are strong waders will be able to reach the runs off the opposite bank. However, the use of a boat is much safer. Unless you survey the water in the daytime to locate the ledges, don't wade boldly in low light. The change from shallow to deep water is abrupt and dangerous to the unwary.

If you find the vanguard of the migration at the Anglers' Access in the first week of September, you can expect good fishing from here to above Spring Creek until the season ends. From the bridge at Chiloquin upstream, you cannot fish from a boat but outboard motors are not allowed. Public access from Chiloquin upstream to Spring Creek is limited. If you are interested in fishing this section, you can drift downstream from Spring Creek and disembark to fish. Some anglers drift downstream from Collier State Park at Spring Creek and paddle back when they finish fishing.

This is best done with a lightweight canoe as the nearest place to put in is 75 yards from the parking area. The current is surprisingly strong and a heavier boat would be difficult to row against the current for the trip back to the put-in.

Despite the private property that lies on either bank of the Williamson River below Spring Creek downstream of the relatively short length of public water, foot access may be available through the Crystalwood Lodge and Bed & Breakfast. This lodge is located on the west side of Klamath Lake at Crystal Springs. The lodge leases property along river corridors in the area, among which is a stretch of the Williamson River above Chiloquin. If you wish to fish this part of the river through the Lodge, you should inquire if this is still offered as leases are granted from year to year.

Fishing can be very good where Spring Creek enters the Williamson River. Collier State Park is located here and many years ago, Chris, Corinna our daughter, and I spent the last two weeks of every October at the campground. When our timing was right, we never moved our camper except to go to town for more supplies. Most of our fishing was done at the confluence and it was outstanding. The rainbows we caught averaged 18 inches. For every rainbow taken of the 12-inch size, we caught one approaching two feet. We used #16 Light Cahills when the rainbows fed on the surface and #16 Gold Ribbed Hare's Ears when nymphing. The major feeding periods in fair weather were from 9:00 to 11:00 in the morning and again from about 4:30 to dark. Overcast days were the exception. Then the fish fed all day. Some years, the air temperature never got much above 32 degrees, the snow stayed on the ground, and the water pipes in the lower campground froze. Through it all, the rainbows still fed with great regularity.

Current weather patterns seem to be less severe with autumns more mild. For this reason, you should pay even more attention to the weather before considering an autumn trip. This is particularly important if you are interested in concentrating on the waters around Spring Creek.

In the autumn, the waters from Spring Creek contribute about half of the volume of the Williamson River at its confluence entering at a constant 43 degrees. A pair of boot-footed neoprene waders is suggested and insulated undergarments will contribute to keeping you warm. To reach all the holding water, you must wade to your waist. The current is not strong and the footing is good, but wading this deep for a couple of hours can cause great discomfort if you are ill prepared.

During the evening rise at the confluence of Spring Creek, Mike landed this rainbow, which took a dry fly.

In addition to the waters at the confluence, a couple more places about three quarters of a mile downstream normally hold fish. You can reach this area by driving back to the highway and heading south. Park at the first pull-out on the river side of the highway. One spot will be marked with a wooden wagon wheel. From here, there is a good pool upstream, back toward Spring Creek, and another just downstream a short distance. Once you come to the fenced property, you cannot proceed any farther downstream by wading.

The campground at Collier State Park is typical of many of the State campgrounds in Oregon. Hot showers, flush toilets and spotless wash basins are what you will find. Years ago, chopped firewood was free, but now you must pay a small fee. Rates are nominal for a tent site or for full hook-ups. Unless you are extremely hardy or the weather is abnormally mild, tent camping is not advised late in the season.

On the dirt road leading upstream from Collier State Park is the upper Williamson River Campground. It was unimproved for many years and free to use, but each site now has a picnic table, a fire pit, and there are outhouses. Off this same road are a number of spurs that take you back to the river. Since this is upstream of the confluence of Spring Creek, the Williamson is much smaller in this stretch. In most autumns, there are schools of rainbows in this section of river and they can be challenging. In the absence of heavy rains, the water is clear and slow moving. This fishing is similar to confronting a very slow moving spring creek and the best approach is to use long leaders and small flies. Pheasant Tail Nymphs in sizes #18 and #20 are good choices. Dark weighted mayfly nymphs in the same size can be good too. After locating a group of fish, a quiet approach is necessary in order to have any chance at all. For spring creek specialists, this fishing will be most interesting.

If you continue on this dirt road past the road leading into the campground, you will eventually cross an old wooden bridge. There are some slow moving pools upstream that are too deep to fish by wading. Downstream of the bridge, where you can park on a bluff, fish can be spotted in a large pool. This is some of the most difficult water to fish because your approach cannot be concealed. Big

fish are often found in this pool, sometimes in large numbers.

The fall rainbows in the Williamson are dark fish with few markings. They are not as beautiful as fully spotted rainbows found in other waters, but they do grow large. I've not been keeping track of how big the largest fish caught of late have been, but ten-pound rainbows are still present. Whether there are still fish exceeding 20 pounds like there once was, is not known to me. These giant rainbows were very rare, but the average size of the Williamson River fish still runs between two and four pounds. The largest I've ever landed was nearly ten pounds taken on a Muddler Minnow. Perhaps one of the reasons why I've not landed larger fish for all the time spent is that I still prefer to fish small dry flies and nymphs the majority of the time. This is where I find the most challenge and satisfaction.

Through the years, Chris and I fished numerous times with Rich Henry, a native Chiloquin Indian. On one trip, he showed us where to find a school of rainbows above the confluence of Spring Creek. Williamson River fish tend to be very gregarious. There were about 75 rainbows in this school running from two to ten pounds. We took several up to a little more than five pounds using small nymphs. Rich used a #18 trico nymph and I chose a #18 Pheasant Tail. The fish held in a pool where the main current, although very slight, separated us from the milling rainbows off the far bank. Rich hooked his fish by casting to the head of the school and mending his line to offset the current's affect. Then he began a very slow retrieve as drag set in. I hooked fish by doing the same, from a more downstream angle, and used an indicator to help identify the strikes.

If you come repeatedly to this area, you will find that fish are not concentrated in the same runs each year. Even when you find large groups of rainbows, they will test the most experienced anglers. Long leaders tapered 6x or even 7x must be employed. For this delicate fishing, #3 and #4 rods are best. Although you might hook a very large fish, their tendency is not to leave the pool. With such light tippets, you can't force the issue anyway. Light, constant pressure will eventually tire any hooked fish.

In the last months of the season, fish will still be coming out of the lake and moving into the lower and mid section of the Williamson. The most popular drift during the warmer months, from the Anglers' Access at Chiloquin to the Highway 97 Bridge, can still fish very well in the autumn. Since many of these fish have been in the river for some time and may have been fished

On the downstream side of the Highway 97 Bridge, the Williamson River flows by the Water Wheel Campground. There is good fishing by the campground, particularly if the summer is warm, driving the rainbows from shallow Klamath Lake to the cool waters of the Williamson River.

over, long casts to 70 and even 80 feet can sometimes mean the difference between just an ordinary day to one worth remembering. For those of above average casting skills, four to six fish a day with a few exceeding five pounds would not be out of the question providing you have a good guide or know exactly where the fish lie.

When Chris and I first came to fish the Williamson, guides were few. Rich Henry was a guide and he had a special way of treating certain clients. If he liked you, he would refuse payment thereafter. Rich was the only guide who took clients to the waters above Spring Creek. There may be some guides who do so now, but I'm unaware of them. If you find you need a guide,

On this drift with Dale, Mike hooked a rainbow that was estimated to weigh around fifteen pounds. It was lost when the fish rolled on the surface and the hook pulled free. This fish being released is fairly typical of the rainbows that inhabit the Williamson River.

results will not be good unless you can cast at least 40 feet. The fear of any guide is to have clients who cannot cast. This is particularly the case on the Williamson where truly trophy rainbows are present and nothing can be done by the guides to guarantee success if you can't put the fly where it needs to be without spooking the fish.

By far, the greatest angling pressure on the Williamson takes place in the summer. If you hire a guide, chances are you will drift from the Anglers' Access at Chiloquin and take out at the Highway 97 Bridge. Except at the start of the drift where there are riffles and lava formations protruding above the surface, the water is a big

meander without much definition. Some refer to it as frog water. Guides drift the river daily and this allows them to keep track of the schools of fish. To those without experience who drift on their own, it would be difficult to know exactly where to fish and concentrate their efforts.

Most of the fish tend to hold near the banks, especially below bends in the stream. The scouring of the water creates more depth. A Type II shooting taper is what I prefer to use, but a sink tip line will also work. Guides will instruct you to cast toward the bank and after your leech or Woolly Bugger has settled a bit, allow the fly to swing away from the bank as you begin a slow retrieve. Most of the strikes will come early in the retrieve to suggest that many of the fish are bank oriented.

On a drift once with Dale Siens, who has since retired from guiding, I got a bit tired from the casting and retrieving and allowed the fly to hang downstream of the boat to give my arm a rest. When I started to retrieve the fly, something felt heavy and I thought I had hooked a clump of weeds. When the object began to move, there was no doubt that a fish had taken my leech. Perhaps the fish was just pricked in the lip because when it surfaced and rolled, showing its broad back and long flank, the fly came free. Dale and I both thought this rainbow was in the 15-pound class, the largest I had ever hooked on the Williamson, but just for a instant.

Afternoon winds that always seem to blow upstream can sometimes be a real drag for drifters. As the river becomes wide and the current slows, it takes a lot of energy to oar the rest of the way to the take out. Some guides carry an electric motor for this reason. Before you reach the Highway 97 Bridge, you will float by Lonesome Duck, the nicest accommodation on the river. The lodge is located on a part of the river that hosts some great Hexegenia hatches in July. Like the hatch of this big mayfly on any stream, it can be better in some years than others. When the hatches are intense and regular, it is something to experience. During years of intense and sustained hatches, the flies keep coming off into August. Once the hatch gets underway and the trout become used to seeing the adults at dusk, they begin to anticipate the big mayflies so much that the rainbows can be tempted to rise an hour before the daily emergence begins.

Dale nets a Williamson rainbow for Mike.

*Mike nets a
Williamson rainbow.*

In the autumn of 1998, Chris and I took the opportunity to visit Lonesome Duck and to fish with guide Ed Miranda Senior. Ed has guided anglers on the Williamson longer than anyone we know. Through the years, he had asked us to come and fish with him on numerous occasions. We finally made the time and on the same trip, Chris and I stayed at Lonesome Duck, a facility comprised of two luxury housekeeping cabins and a restored cottage with an impressive stone fireplace. Some of our readers have reported to us that they have enjoyed staying here.

In the late afternoon, Chris and I arrived to the west side of Klamath Lake by Rocky Point where Ed Miranda and his wife, Bernie, reside. They have another home a few lots away, which they used previously to put up anglers and hunters. After the fishing season comes to a close, Ed guides waterfowl shooters. The rental house where we stayed is no longer available. Ed may be able to recommend lodging nearby. Other than the motel rooms at Rocky Point Resort, there are no other places offering lodging at reasonable prices in this immediate area. There is a restaurant at the resort, but Ed and Bernie invited us to have dinner with them. The following day, Ed would guide us on the Williamson River.

The day broke clear without any promise of inclement weather. As we mentioned previously, in order to have a mass migration of rainbows move into the upper Williamson from Klamath Lake in the autumn, there must be freezing weather. Prior to our arrival, the weather was way too mild. As a result, runs of rainbows were scarce and scattered. This made the fishing difficult and far less productive than it could be in the presence of cold and foul weather. Although freezing weather was now here, the season ending date of October 31 was only days away. Ed said the regular drift from the Anglers' Access below Chiloquin down to Highway 97 was producing only small fish. If we wanted a chance for bigger rainbows, he suggested we try a stretch of river above town. The odds of catching fish were less in this section, but we choose it anyway because bigger rainbows are always our objective when fishing the Williamson.

Ed said there was no hurry to fish early the next day. The fish didn't become active until after midmorning so we stopped at Miletas Cafe for breakfast before continuing to the stream. At 9:30, Ed led the way towing his boat as we followed in our van conversion. He drove through Chiloquin and then north onto Pine Road where a new subdivision is being developed. Just to the north of the lots, we drove onto land belonging to a friend of Ed's to launch. The Williamson is wide

and shallow at this spot looking as promising as a western trout stream could possibly look. Downstream just a short distance, we could see several big rainbows holding by some sunken logs. The water was clear as glass and the fish looked like they would be difficult to entice. Ed said we would head upstream and return later for a shot at these fish.

To power his drift boat, Ed used a 55-pound thrust Minn Kota electric motor. It moved the heavy boat with ease, even through runs where the flow was constricted and moving at maximum velocity. As we motored upstream, Ed told us there were several schools of rainbows we could approach. As we hugged the right bank at a widening in the river, he said there was a group of about 25 fish off the opposite bank. A half of a mile farther, we came to a spot where a reef nearly broke the surface causing the water to well up. Just downstream from this break, a fish boiled on the surface. Ed motored to a point 150 feet above the school and lowered the anchor. He said the best thing to do was to wait and watch, allowing the wake from the boat to subside. These fish were going to be difficult.

After ten minutes had passed, I disembarked and waded quietly downstream until my position was about 50 feet above where we saw the fish show. For 15 minutes, I waited and watched. The fish didn't rise again. Returning to the boat, I traded the outfit with the floating line and a dry for a #7 outfit with a Type II shooting taper and a weighted leech. After covering the water thoroughly with the submerged fly without any strikes, I returned to the boat and we drifted downstream. Clearly seen in the deep water below the reef were about a dozen rainbows weighing anywhere from two to six pounds. They scattered as we drifted over them.

Ed said the next spot always held fish. Here a ledge forced the main flow toward the opposite bank. We were told the rainbows held on the edge of the ledge just off the main flow or in the deep, slow moving pool off to the side. After the boat was anchored, Chris gained a good spot on the bank to take photographs while Ed and I got into position to cover the water with identical leech patterns. He fished the ledge with a Type II weight forward line and I chose a Scientific Anglers Stillwater to cover the pool.

Ten minutes went by before there was any action. A rainbow took Ed's leech, but the hook didn't take hold. The fly was one he showed me the evening before and of which I had made some copies. When another ten minutes passed without any interest from the trout, I switched to a #10

Bead Head Golden Stonefly Nymph designed by Mike Mercer of The Fly Shop. From where Ed stood, he could see some fish milling near the bottom of the pool next to the current. After making a long cast, I allowed the nymph to sink while counting slowly to 25 before beginning a retrieve. After each ten three-inch strips, I'd pause before starting another sequence. Halfway back, my fly stopped. It proved to be a 22-inch rainbow still carrying warm water lice it had picked up in the lake. The fight was not as spirited as it could have been and the fish was quickly landed and released. We fished for another hour without getting a strike. Every now and then, a fish would roll on the surface.

Downstream at the next spot, we waited in the boat after anchoring to allow the fish to become settled. On the flat across from us a few fish began to rise. We spread out, trying to find a regular feeder. No sooner had we got into position when a breeze came up and the trout stopped rising. Ed was using a nymph and had a strike. This rainbow was a couple of inches larger than the one I landed earlier and it fought well.

It was now about 4:00, just enough time to return to where we launched and try for the fish we saw earlier. When we got back, there was unfortunately an angler casting to these fish. He was working on the land development and taking a break. Although he was about to leave, the fish were now too wary and impossible to catch. We said good-bye to Ed and thanked him for his expert guiding, then headed for Lonesome Duck.

The two luxury cabins and restored cottage that make up Lonesome Duck are situated on a mile and a half of river frontage about two miles upstream of the Highway 97 bridge. Diane Patton, the manager and chef, was there to greet us as we drove up. If you were familiar with the Williamson, you would recognize the water as one of the prime stretches to fish the Hex hatch in July. The property is ideally situated so that if you made the popular drift from the Angler's Access below Chiloquin, you could end your drift at Lonesome Duck. For most of the year, especially if the summer is warm and driving the rainbows out of Klamath Lake, there will be good populations of rainbows at the doorstep of your cabin if you were staying at Lonesome Duck.

As Diane was telling us about the facility, a big rainbow rolled on the surface opposite of our cabin. This was almost enough to make me grab my rod, but it was getting bitterly cold, as the sun had set. Later that evening, we learned from the guest diary that some anglers had caught big rainbows up to nine pounds only two weeks earlier.

Rich plays a rainbow that was hooked on a tiny nymph.

For two days, we rested in the comfort of our two-story cabin and let the world slide by. Steve and Debbie Hilbert are the owners of Lonesome Duck. Debbie is an interior decorator and her distinctive touches are evident. When we did venture out to see the rest of the grounds, the ranch hands asked if we might want to make a short drift from the top of the property. If so, they would load one of the prams or canoes available to guests onto a truck and shuttle us upstream. We decided just to paddle a pram to the other side of the river to take a few photos.

With three cabins, Lonesome Duck can sleep up to 16 guests. A number of groups have taken over the entire facility and have had Diane cook for them. Diane is a former restaurant owner and chef. She wanted to cook a meal for us, but we had brought along so much food that we declined. On the back porch of each cabin is a gas barbecue and the kitchens are fully equipped so all guests have to do is to bring food, unless of course, you want Diane to take care of your meals.

In our travels, we come upon places that we wish we could visit more often. Our work doesn't allow this because we need to be on the move constantly to find new places for our readers to visit. Lonesome Duck is a place where we would like to spend more time. Given a choice, I'd choose the time for our visit from early July through mid August. If the Hex hatch happens, we'd be right in the heart of the best water. It would only be a short drive to the lower Wood where big rainbows might be rising to hoppers. Lonesome Duck is centrally located so anglers can fish anywhere in the Klamath Lake basin. Of course, it is also a perfect place to relax and do very little.

At almost any time during the season, and especially in the summer and early fall, good-sized rainbows can be found at the Anglers's Access.

SUMMARY

For those who like to fish for large, wild rainbows, the Williamson River offers some that can weigh more than ten pounds. There are a growing number of guides in the area, but only a handful with long-time experience. The most opportune time to fish is when the stream first settles down from spring run off, during July and early August if the *Hexegenia* hatch is in progress and then in mid September through October if fish have migrated to the upper river by Spring Creek. Please remember, the fishing is not easy and you cannot expect to do well if you possess less than average abilities, even when hiring a guide. Check the weather report in Klamath Falls to make sure cool weather has set in before making an autumn trip. Temperatures are listed in many newspapers or can be found by calling the Klamath Falls Herald & News at (541/885-4410). The town of Chiloquin has a few eating establishments and a market should you need supplies. The hardware store is well stocked with outdoor equipment and sells fishing licenses.

Fly Shops & Guides

• WILLIAMSON RIVER ANGLERS, PO Box 669, Jct. Hwys. 97 & 62, Chiloquin, OR, 97624; Tel. 541-783-2677, is the only fly shop in the area. The shop acts as an agent for many of the flyfishing guides in the area, including Ed Miranda Sr., and Ed Miranda, Jr. We can recommend both of the Mirandas from personal experience. For more information about the Klamath Lake basin, refer to Volume IV, #1, January 15, 1995.

• ED A. MIRANDA SR., Box 522 Fort Klamath, Oregon 97626; Tel. 541-381-2266, FAX 541-381-2222, Guides anglers and waterfowl hunters through-out the Klamath Lake basin. Rates are $160/person/day, for two or more anglers $320/day, $250 half-day for one or two people. He guides for Lonesome Duck also.

Motels

• LONESOME DUCK, PO Box 8164, Incline Village, NV, 89452; Tel. 800-367-2540, website: lonesomeduck.com, e-mail: steveh@lonesomeduck.com, is comprised of two luxury, housekeeping cabins and a restored cottage fronting a mile and a half of the Williamson River upstream of the Highway 97 bridge. The cabins (River's Edge and Eagle's Nest) have similar floor plans with a bedroom downstairs, a bedroom upstairs plus a sleeping loft, a full kitchen, two full baths and a living area. The Arrowhead cottage is a single level with two bedrooms, and it's more intimate. It was the original ranch house, named for the arrowheads embedded in the fireplace. Boats and canoes are available for rent, but the next time we make a visit, Chris and I will bring our own prams and electric motors because we are more familiar with them. The rates for double occupancy for Eagle's Nest and River's Edge were $250/night. For Arrowhead Cottage, it was $200/night. Boat rental was $40/day and canoes rented for $25/day. Half-day rentals were less. Dinners were $30/person and required two-week's notice. Breakfast and boxed lunches were also available at $12.50 each. Lonesome Duck is suitable for large parties, small groups and individuals. Of all the possible accommodations in the area, Lonesome Duck is the only one situated on the Williamson River where you can catch large rainbows almost at your door.

• MELITAS MOTEL & CAFE, 39500 Highway 97 North, Chiloquin, OR, 97624. Tel. 541-783-2401, has clean rooms for around $40/single and $55/double. The food served in the cafe is okay.

• THE SPRING CREEK RANCH MOTEL, HC 63, Box 440, Chiloquin, OR, 97624; Tel. 541-783-2775, is at the headwaters of Spring Creek. It has ten units, three motel-like rooms and seven kitchenettes. The prices range from about $28 for one person in a room to $34 for two people in a kitchenette. This complex, built in the 50's, is off the highway and away from road noise.

• THE RAPIDS MOTEL, 33551 Highway 97 North, Chiloquin, OR, 97624; Tel. 541-783-2271, has older, but clean rooms. A single is about $23; for two beds, it's $33. There are ten units in the complex, which normally fills during holiday and it is located right next to the Rapid's Cafe.

• CRYSTALWOOD LODGE, BED & BREAKFAST, P.O. Box 1117 Klamath Falls, Oregon 97601 Tel. 866-381-2322, e-mail: info@crystalwoodlodge.com, website: www.crystalwoodlodge.com. Flyfishing and lodging package: 2 days/3 nights $755/person double occupancy all meals included. Flyfishing guide service by Native Run Flyfishing. It is adjacent to the Upper Klamath Wildlife Refuge overlooking the headwaters of Crystal Creek.

Travel

• HORIZON AIRLINES, a part of ALASKA AIRLINES, Tel. 800-252-7522, services Klamath Falls with a connecting flight out of Portland, Oregon. Vehicles can be rented at the airport. For those with their own light planes, there is a landing strip off Highway 97 just north of the road leading to Chiloquin. Lonesome Duck will pick up guests free of charge, and the Mirandas charge a nominal fee. It is possible to walk across the road from the airstrip to Melitas.

Camping

• COLLIER STATE PARK, is located at the confluence of Spring Creek. There is a day-use picnic area adjacent to the highway and a campground with hook ups. Rates for tent sites and RVs are moderate. The confluence can be a good place to fish at different times during the season.

• WATERWHEEL CAMPGROUND, 200 Williamson River Drive, Chiloquin, OR, 97624; Tel. 541-783-2738, is located just downstream of the bridge that crosses Highway 97 by the Rapid's Cafe. Full hook-ups are $19/day for two people with an additional charge of $1 for each extra person over two years of age. If you only need water and electricity, the charge is $12/day. Tent campers are charged $15/day. There are two 23-foot trailers for rent and they go for $32/day plus tax. The trailers are fully self-contained with air conditioners and very clean. We prefer them to any of the local motels, but you must bring your own bedding or sleeping bag. One of the most productive runs on the lower river borders the campground. Website: www.boatescape.com

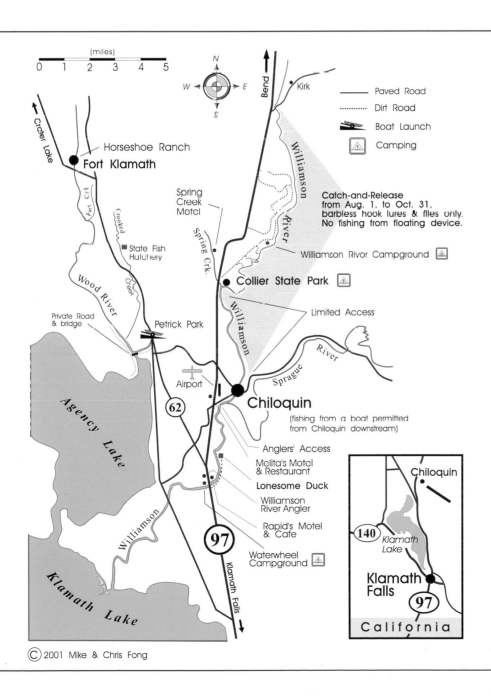

© 2001 Mike & Chris Fong

MISSOURI RIVER

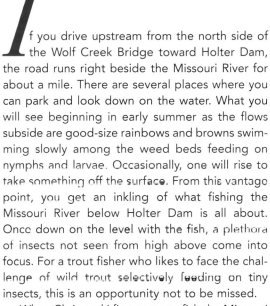

8 *West Central Montana*

MISSOURI RIVER

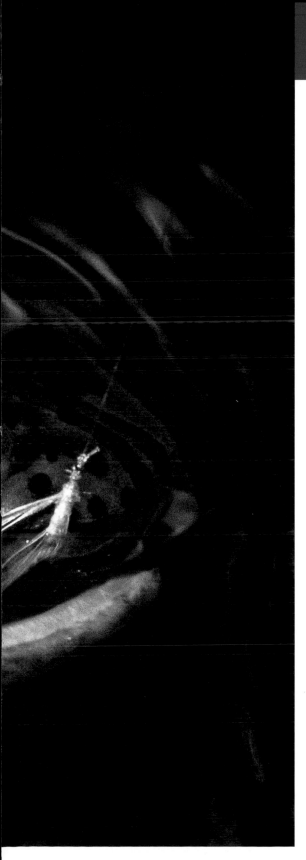

*I*f you drive upstream from the north side of the Wolf Creek Bridge toward Holter Dam, the road runs right beside the Missouri River for about a mile. There are several places where you can park and look down on the water. What you will see beginning in early summer as the flows subside are good-size rainbows and browns swimming slowly among the weed beds feeding on nymphs and larvae. Occasionally, one will rise to take something off the surface. From this vantage point, you get an inkling of what fishing the Missouri River below Holter Dam is all about. Once down on the level with the fish, a plethora of insects not seen from high above come into focus. For a trout fisher who likes to face the challenge of wild trout selectively feeding on tiny insects, this is an opportunity not to be missed.

When Chris and I first came to fish the Missouri in the mid 80s, it was during a series of low-water years. Rainbows gathered in huge schools numbering as many as 300 to 400 individuals to feed collectively on the surface as millions of Tricorythodes mayflies fell from the sky. After the daily midmorning mating flight was finished, many of the fallen flies were trapped in eddies forming carpets that spun around and around like a slow-moving washing machine and the feeding orgy by the trout continued. Throughout the day, different insects appeared and although the surface feeding by the trout was not as intense as during the Trico spinner fall, there were still plenty of trout to be caught using dry flies. Then in the evening, a blizzard of caddis hovered over the water and the trout would feed heavily off the surface until it became too dark to see.

As summer moved into fall, the voracious feeding of the trout continued, only the insects on which they fed were different. After the first frost, hoppers, beetles and ants would no longer be seen, but they wouldn't be missed as Baetis

The spent flies are small and best imitated with flies tied on size 20 hooks. This rainbow fell for a henwing spinner.

Wild Missouri River rainbows are not long lived. Most of the adult fish measure between fourteen and nineteen inches with maximum growth around twenty-five inches. These rainbows are very strong and any fish sixteen inches or larger will usually take all the fly line off the reel and get into the backing.

hatches intensified joined by midges and other invertebrates. This would also be the time when fishing streamers was an excellent choice for those looking to hook the largest rainbows and browns. Into winter it would still be possible to find fish feeding off the surface, but by then most anglers couldn't endure the bitter cold allowing the trout in the stream to feed undisturbed.

The chance to fish exclusively with dry flies depends on several factors. Without regards to the insects themselves, it is moderate or reduced flows that allow surface feeding to be sustained. This is the reason why western spring creeks with their constant flows are so perfect for fishing with

the predominant rainbows don't grow extremely large with a twenty-five-inch fish hovering near maximum growth, their strength and speed could be favorably compared to the fight of steelhead. During flows of 5,000 cfs or less, the bottom of pea gravel is easy to wade and for drifters, there are no rapids except for the shallow water flowing under the freeway bridge as one leaves behind the mountains and drops down onto the plains. As with most tailwater fisheries, the highest concentrations of fish are found in the upper reaches toward the dam. Expect to encounter the most anglers from the dam down to Craig, the most

The Missouri River flowing from Holter Dam is closely followed by Interstate 15. For the entire distance down to Cascade, the stream supports trout.

dry flies or by sight-fishing with small nymphs. The Missouri below Holter Dam is like a gigantic spring creek, but only in those years following mild winters when precipitation is within normal ranges. This was certainly the case as recently as in 1999, which followed three heavy winters influenced by the effects of El Niño. Some anglers referred to the dry-fly fishing on the Missouri in 1999 to be "just like the good old days," forgetting that there have been far more years of exceptional dry-fly fishing in the last ten years than when one was forced to fish beneath the surface for good results.

The Missouri River below Holter Dam is a stream Chris and I would fish every year as long as flows were conducive for dry-fly fishing. Although

popular take-out for drifters starting either at the dam or at Wolf Creek Bridge. If crowds are a co cern, be aware that there are good populations of trout all the way down to Cascade, a distance of about thirty-five miles. On our July/August visit in 1999, we found excellent fishing on the weekend in spite of the crowds. By mid week, 90% of the anglers were gone and fishing was "like the good old days." Our report on the Missouri River below Holter dam appeared in Volume I, Number 3, March 1992. It is updated here to reflect changes of which we are now aware.

MISSOURI RIVER

*I*n the second issue of The Inside Angler, we published a report on the Missouri River below

Holter Dam in Montana. Since then, Chris and I have fished this stretch of the stream numerous times. The reason for this is simple; of all the tail-water fisheries in the West, it remains one of our favorites. In spite of a growing number of anglers, it retains what we found so attractive during our first visit sixteen years ago. The stream is readily accessible, wading is easy, the fishing for its wild rainbow and brown trout is challenging and the fish themselves are wonderful. They are what connoisseurs of stream-born trout wish some other western tailwater fisheries had; fish perfectly suited to a stream that were naturally evolved and able to sustain themselves.

Our most recent visit took place two years ago. We met Jim Crawford, TIA correspondent, at the Missouri River Trout Shop and Lodge on Friday, July 16, where we had rooms reserved. Jim makes his home in Polson, Montana and had never fished the Missouri. Besides wanting to visit with Jim and to introduce him to the stream, we had arranged to fish with Tim Plaska of Missouri River Expeditions and to become familiar with Wolf Creek Lodge. We met Tim at the International Sportsmen's Exposition in San Francisco where he had a booth. He told us about Wolf Creek Lodge, a place that some of our subscribers might find of interest in staying.

After having lunch at the Trout Shop Cafe, Jim put his gear in our van and we headed upstream. It was breezy, but we could see some rises downstream along the east bank as we drove across the bridge at Craig. Farther up the road, at an anglers' access, we stopped to look at the stream from a point high above the water. There were several anglers fishing around an island, but no one where the water dropped into a deep pool. We could see several good-size rainbows nymphing and rising sporadically, including one that looked to be around five pounds. It was almost enough to tempt us into stopping here to fish. We continued on.

At the Wolf Creek Bridge, the parking lot was half filled. Most of the vehicles were hitched to empty boat trailers. There were also some RVs and a few house trailers set up looking like they were going to stay for a while. This is the starting point for the most popular drift on the river ending at Craig. Before reaching the bridge, a road to the left goes along the north side of the river. Along this road, fish rose here and there in spite of gusting winds. After driving past Rainbow Island, the road veered away from the stream and started to rise toward Holter Lake. For years, the restaurant at Holter Lake Lodge served the best dinners in the area. It was under different

ownership and we stopped to see if the menu had changed. In the restaurant, we ran into several acquaintances and they said the food was good.

We drove back downstream looking for an unoccupied place to fish. At a spot where several good-size trout were feeding off a weed bed close to shore, we pulled off the road and parked. It wouldn't be easy to fish here because there

After the flies mate, they fall to the water and trout feed heavily on them. The mating lasts about two hours each morning providing an extended feeding period for the trout and a good opportunity for anglers to imitate the fallen naturals with dry flies.

wasn't much room between the river's edge and a steep cliff. When we made our way down to the water, the fish nearby sensed our presence and quit rising. We spread out and waited.

From 3:30 to 7:00, fish rose sporadically to emerging caddis, PMDs and smaller bugs I couldn't identify. You could tell by the splashy rises when the moth-like insects were being taken. This comes about when trout chase the swimming pupae and take them at the surface. Because the rocky and uneven bottom dropped off quickly, it wasn't safe to wade too far from the bank. This restricted our backcasts. What was even more excruciating was a strong upstream wind. This made it extremely difficult to set up for drag-free drifts and refusals were the rule of the day. Most of the time, we couldn't even cast until there was a lull between the strong gusts. By the end of the session, each of us had landed one trout. Chris' was a seventeen-inch rainbow taken on a #16 PMD; Jim netted an eighteen-inch brown that fell for a #16 Elk Hair Caddis; and I took a fifteen-inch brown on a #18 Green Sparkle Dun. We had other fish on, including a couple of good-size rainbows that streaked toward the middle of the river, buried themselves in weeds and broke off 6x tippets. It was a frustrating afternoon.

We ate dinner at the Trout Shop and found that the food was well prepared. The cook was a good-natured fellow named Mark, an avid angler. When he isn't busy filling orders, you might ask him what the trout are attracted to at the moment. He'll know. All the rooms at the lodge were taken. The complex remains the most popular hangout on the river. Just about everyone not

Spent flies collect in eddies where trout feed on them by taking mouthfuls at a time. This fishing looks easy, but it isn't. The flies swirl in irregular patterns and the trout move back and forth in the current presenting moving targets.

staying at another lodge comes to the Trout Shop to eat, buy flyfishing supplies or just to see who might be dropping by. The most popular campground, because of its central location, is across the road beyond the boat launch. A few years ago, the Trout Shop moved its fly shop into a building across the street where the Parrot Fly Shop used to be. This made it possible to expand the cafe for more seating and to enlarge the kitchen. It was a welcomed renovation.

We met Tim Plaska, our guide, in the cafe at 7:30 for breakfast. While eating, Tim suggested that we should fish downstream to get away from the majority of the weekend traffic. There were clouds to the west, no wind, and the day looked promising. We made sure we had our rain jackets in our dry bag before launching at 9:30. Chris and I still recalled a beautiful morning on the Missouri when we didn't bring our raingear and ended up getting drenched.

After drifting for a quarter of a mile, Tim beached the dory so we could fish on foot by an island. There were some PMDs and caddis on the water, but only a few fish were rising. I started with a PMD Sparkle Dun tied the evening before. Jim took a position at the head of the run, while Tim worked with Chris and me further downstream. As Tim set Chris up with a #16 PMD trailing a #18 Green Bead Head Caddis on a three-foot dropper, I saw a trout rise twice. This gave me a target. On the third cast, it rose confidently to my fly and the fight was on. Missouri rainbows are known for their strength and speed. This one showed its stuff as it quickly got into my backing. Only after I was able to steer the rainbow into the slowed water below the island could it be subdued. We estimated its length between eighteen and nineteen inches.

After we resumed fishing, a trout took Chris' bead head. It had to be a good-size rainbow because it streaked off on a spool-spinning run. Chris tried to slow it down and all that became of this was the parting of the 5x tippet. After this, we couldn't find any more risers on this side of the island, so we went to see if any trout were working on the other side. There were only a couple. Soon more PMDs were on the water promoting more fish to rise. Between the three of us, we couldn't draw a strike. We asked Tim to give it a try. He got three trout to rise, landing one about sixteen inches. The reason he succeeded where we failed was that he was able to get longer drag-free drifts. This was accomplished by wading out further above the fish thereby positioning himself so drag from cross currents would be less influential.

For most of the day, we had steady, but not fast, fishing. We fished by wading and from the boat. At 1:00, Tim set up a folding table and some chairs on a rock bar for a sumptuous, health-conscious lunch. As we ate, a few fish rose. Late in the afternoon, it started to cloud up. We had thunder, lightning and a few sprinkles. Before this, we had our best luck using #14 Elk Hair Caddis. A lot of tan-colored caddis were flying above the water, but we didn't see many actually on the surface. We took out at 7:00. For the last hour, it was mainly a boat ride as the trout became inactive. For the day, our total number of trout landed was seventeen, all rainbows. As you would expect, we had strikes from trout that we didn't hook and some got off before they were landed. The largest trout was the one I landed at the beginning of the drift.

There were several things that stood out while making this drift on the lower river toward Cascade. If your preference is to fish dry flies, it's best to spot good-size trout and then concentrate on catching this individual before moving on. Most of the larger fish fed along the banks. It was not effective to fish by just casting to likely-looking water. This fishing was more like what you find on a spring creek where trout come to the surface only when duns or spinners are on the water. Contrary to this and perhaps particular to the Missouri, there were times when many PMDs were on the water and few, if any, trout rose. When the first PMDs appear in early June, trout don't hesitate to take them and do so vigorously. When the PMD hatches become regular, they are joined by such a profusion of other aquatic insects that the trout can become indifferent. If fish are feeding and ignore surface offerings, use a Bead Head Nymph on a three-foot dropper. When fish aren't showing at all, fish streamers or Woolly Buggers on sinking lines. Some of the largest trout taken on the Missouri fall to the latter.

Of the six rooms at the Missouri River Trout Shop and Lodge, three have private baths. The studio apartment upstairs has two queen beds, a roll out, a kitchen area and bathroom. On Saturday night, the patrons of the bar next door can get awfully loud. The guests in the apartment above our room returned after 2:00. They made so much noise before turning in that they woke us up. It would be nice if the lodge would notify people staying upstairs to be more considerate of those staying in the rooms below. Also, a train came by sometime in the middle of the night. I'm

As dusk approaches, three anglers wait on the bank while another begins to cast to fish that are starting to rise.

a light sleeper and those who sleep more soundly might not have noticed.

On Sunday, we got to the river around 9:30. We were on foot and chose to fish across from the mouth of Prickley Pear Creek. A Trico spinner fall was in progress, but not with the intensity to blanket the water. There was the usual array of different bugs on the water and the fish were making sipping rises, like they do when taking spinners. At 11:30, a steady breeze came up and the trout stopped rising. Before this, there were not a lot of active fish, but enough to give us some targets. During our session, a steady stream of boats went by. At one time, eight were in view. Chris landed the nicest trout on a #20 Trico Sparkle Dun, a nineteen-inch brown. Jim hooked several fish on a small caddis, but didn't land any. I only hooked one, which took a Caddis Emerger. It buried itself in a clump of weeds that was floating by, breaking the tippet.

For the next two nights, we stayed at Wolf Creek Lodge. This newly-built luxury housekeeping home sits on a hill with a commanding view of the river. It's located upstream of the Wolf Creek Bridge on the south side of the stream. From the porch outside the living room/dining/kitchen area, we could see fish rising on the river through a telescope. The kitchen has all the modern

Guide Tim Plaska displays a rainbow that Chris took on a small dry fly.

Good numbers of brown trout are found in the stream, but their numbers are far less than the rainbows.

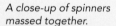

A close-up of spinners massed together.

conveniences. On this floor are the master bedroom with a private bath and Jacuzzi, and a guest bathroom. Upstairs are a loft with a couch, an entertainment center with two comfortable, stuffed chairs and a writing desk with a chair. Downstairs you'll find a bathroom and two bedrooms with sliding doors leading to a large hot tub. A southwest/western theme is echoed in the furnishings and the lighting hardware is especially interesting with hints of The Arts & Crafts Movement. Wildlife reliefs are incorporated into the chandeliers and lamps. This is a "dream" house as far as Chris and I are concerned.

We fished this evening with Tim, making a short drift from the dam down to Wolf Creek Bridge. Shortly after launching at 7:30, we came upon a blizzard of caddis. In spite of caddis choking the air, few fish rose. There were a good number of anglers wade fishing both sides of the stream. At the lower end of Rainbow Island, Tim beached the boat to see if any sustained feeding would develop. Soon the wind began to subside and fish started to rise. It was one of those evenings when it would get calm for a while and then the wind would start up again making fishing a dry difficult. Jim was the top rod, hooking seven rainbows on a #10 Green Shrimp pattern fished on a wet-fly swing. I stayed with a dry and hooked three trout, managing only to land a twelve-incher. Right near dark, Chris landed a nineteen-inch rainbow, which put up a tremendous battle before being netted by Tim.

By the time we returned to Wolf Creek Lodge, Pam, Tim's wife, had dinner started. We had a feast of steaks and country-style spare ribs, which Pam seasoned and I barbecued on a gas grill on the front porch. To go along with the meat, we had corn on the cob, baked potatoes, garlic bread, a green salad and a couple of bottles of wine brought from home. If guests prefer not to cook, food can be prepared at the Trout Shop Cafe and delivered. The charge for delivering is minimal. It was an evening filled with lots of laughs and fish talk.

When I got up at 6:30, Jim had already left for home because of a pressing appointment. A note on the table thanked us for the good time. He also wrote that fish were already rising. After Chris woke up and we had a bowl of cereal and some fruit, we went again to the stream near Prickley Pear Creek, arriving at 8:15. Only one boat was in sight. Fish were already rising.

On the second cast, I landed an eighteen-inch rainbow on a #18 Rusty Spinner. As Chris worked to a pod of fish, I saw a number of trout downstream where a bar slowed the current by a small cove. There were five or six risers feeding close together. I managed to put all of them down with one cast. The only excitement I had here was to watch a rattlesnake swim close by and slither onto the bank. Working my way back up toward Chris, I saw a solitary fish feeding one foot off the bank. It must have taken this feeding position after I passed by earlier. Every now and then, it would move laterally away from the bank to take something off the surface and then return to its lie. It was either a large rainbow, or possibly a brown. I made what I thought was the perfect presentation timed to when the trout moved away from the bank to feed. It wasn't good enough from my downstream position. Without a wake, the fish vanished, just like bonefish sometimes do. Chris then hooked a strong fish, that ran downstream. As she waded past in pursuit, I went up to cast to the pod. We soon had a double. Chris' took a gray/yellow CDC and mine took a fresh Rusty Spinner. Chris' was around eighteen inches, slightly larger than the one I landed.

On the day before, it was impractical to fish a fly beneath the surface because there were clumps of weeds continuously floating by, probably broken away by boaters dropping and weighing anchors and numerous wading anglers. There were less weeds on this day so I decided to try a #16 Olive Caddis Emerger because some of the rises were of the splashy kind. It didn't take long to hook a fish, but it sure took a while to land it. From where the fly was taken, I had to follow it downstream more than 125 yards to finish the battle. While fighting this twenty-one-inch rainbow, Chris hooked up again. We had another double. Now it was near 11:00 and the morning rise was coming to an end. I landed one more rainbow measuring ten inches. It was good to see it wasn't affected by whirling disease recently detected in Prickly Pear Creek.

It had been a wonderful morning of fishing. The only negative was the presence of deer flies. They weren't bad when we were on the water, but while walking back to the van they became a nuisance. Our insect repellent was left in our vehicle.

We stopped at the Trout Shop to buy some ice cream to make coke floats planning to return to the lodge to eat and rest. At the Wolf Creek Bridge, we decided first to go upstream to see if any fish were still feeding. Unlike the previous days, there was no wind to speak of. There were far fewer anglers on the stream, this being a weekday. One angler was fishing at a place that provided us with an interesting perspective. From our high vantage point, we could see how trout responded to his dry fly. It was intriguing. At this spot, it was possible to wade out from the bank and make presentations quartering downstream to the trout strung along the bank. This is the preferred angle for casting to trout on flat flows because the fly can be presented ahead of the leader.

At the start, some of the trout would inspect the fly as it drifted past. It looked like a few of them almost took the fly, but refused at the last second when drag set in. The angler was never aware that trout even looked at his fly. He probably thought his choice of fly was incorrect. As the angler continued to fish, the trout he cast to earlier remained where they were, they just refused to rise. Some even continued feeding on nymphs. Downstream other trout rose. From the water, it would have been reasonable to think that the fish cast to earlier were slowly dropping downstream. This has always been my thinking. Considering what we saw, the next time I'm in this situation, I'm going to try to be more patient. If fish refuse because I couldn't extend my drag-free drift, I'll rest the fish for a full five minutes to see if they resume rising. Then I'll try again. If they fail to come to the surface, I'll switch to a #20 Pheasant Tail nymph and fish it with a small yarn indicator two to three feet above the fly. I'd fish it the same way as I would a dry, trying to drift it drag free. There is no doubt that these fish want to feed, which makes them vulnerable.

After resting and enjoying the comforts of the lodge, we ate dinner at 6:00. Chris suggested that we fish this evening at Rainbow Island. When we drove by, there were already four anglers positioned around the island. We continued upstream and parked on the bluff upstream. After getting into our waders, we began descending on the path. At the lower parking area were three vehicles we hadn't seen from above. On the stream three gentlemen sat on the bank looking out to the river. It was dead calm and lots of fish were rising regularly. Since it appeared they were going to remain in this spot, Chris and I headed upstream.

The fish were in small pods feeding close to the bank. In the low flows, it wasn't necessary to wade out more than knee deep to get above rising fish. I had the caddis emerger tied on left over from the morning fishing. For fifteen minutes, I used it because some of the rises were splashy. I

didn't have a touch. By watching carefully, I could see some of the trout take small cream-colored mayflies. Immediately after tying on a #18 PMD, I had a take. While leading the fish to net after a lengthy struggle, the hook pulled free. Minutes later, I hooked another trout. From the way it fought, it seemed pretty good sized and it came off too. It was now 8:45 and the trout quit feeding on the small mayfly. They were sipping so I tied on a Rusty Spinner. I swear I had a couple of takes, but didn't feel a fish either time. By 9:00, the larger fish that were showing earlier quit feeding. There were still packs of smaller fish roaming about and I missed a strike with a Green LaFontaine Caddis Emerger. For the next twenty minutes until 9:30, when we stopped fishing, I didn't touch a fish in spite of lots of surface feeding. The air was swarming with caddis and some mosquitoes. Repellent kept the mosquitoes away, but the caddis engulfed us. They were everywhere, between our glasses and in our ears making loud buzzing sounds. We didn't remove our gear until we returned to the lodge.

The next morning, there was hardly a soul on the river. There were a few clouds in the sky and the fish were rising. If we weren't scheduled to be somewhere else in the afternoon, we would have stayed to fish. It was hard to leave.

This scene of the Missouri River by Rainbow Island was taken years ago when far fewer anglers came to fish. In spite of increasing numbers of flyfishers, the quality of the dry-fly fishing remains very high.

SUMMARY

Fishing the Missouri River below Holter Dam remains a unique flyfishing experience, especially for anglers who like to fish dry flies on flat flows for selective wild trout. After our visit, the Trico spinner falls became more intense and the fish began to feed in large pods. Anglers with long-time experience on the stream said it was like fishing in the "old days." As the summer wore on, the flows were reduced to 4,300 cfs, a level that made wading on the pea-gravel bottom as easy as it gets. Each year, the flow regimen is different. For 1999, it was "normal" or slightly below normal. In years like this, especially following years of higher flows, the fish population becomes optimum for numbers and size of trout. Dry-fly fishing is prime once the flows drop down to 5,500 cfs. In high-water years, flows may not reach this level and as a result, the fish are less likely to feed off the surface.

The rainbows of the Missouri are not long lived. They don't get as large as fish in some other streams. Any fish over twenty inches is considered large. During our visit, it was reported that a twenty-five-inch rainbow was landed on a trico spinner imitation. This was an extraordinary feat, and not just for the angler. For a Missouri rainbow to attain that size, it had to be close to as big as it would get.

During August and early September, fishing terrestrials becomes popular. Caddis and mayfly hatches remain, and you may even encounter good numbers of aquatic moths. Once the weather becomes cool, Baetis hatches can blanket the water. We have seen some of the most intense Baetis emergences on the Missouri while it was snowing. In the cold, they linger on the water longer, promoting great dry-fly fishing. At this time the lower river sees an influx of out-of-area guides who come primarily to fish streamers and Woolly Buggers for the big browns in the lower river. Because of a growing number of anglers, something unavoidable on most quality western streams, I strongly suggest visiting during the week and not on the weekend. There are no rapids to speak of, and if you own a personal inflatable this is a gentle river to float.

Businesses

Listed below are businesses mentioned in the report and others we have enjoyed or inspected previously. In addition, there are other places to stay, eating establishments and guides in the area unfamiliar to us.

• TIM PLASKA, MISSOURI RIVER EXPEDITIONS, 3 LAVA MOUNTAIN COURT NORTH, CLANCY, MT 59634 Tel. 406-449-6446, e-mail: tim@MissouriRiverExp.com, website: MissouriRiverExp.com, provides guiding and outfitting on a number of Montana rivers including the Missouri, the Blackfoot, Dearborn, the Sun and Big Hole. Arrangements can be made through Missouri River Expeditions for day fishing at the H Lazy 6 Ranch near Choteau and the Heaven on Earth Ranch south of Ulm. A rod fee of $100/person is charged to fish these ranches and guiding is extra. For guided drift fishing, the rate is $300 per day for one or two anglers. This includes guided float fishing, flies, snacks, beverages and a streamside lunch. A $100 deposit is required when making reservations. Overnight trips are available.

• MISSOURI RIVER TROUT SHOP AND LODGE, Craig Route, Craig, MT 59648; Tel. 800-337-8528, 406-235-4474, FAX 406-235-4077, e-mail: flyshop@thetroutshop.com, web site: thetrout-shop.com, has guest rooms, a studio apartment, a complete fly shop with boats for rent and shuttle service, a cafe on the premises, rents riverside cabins and acts as a booking agent for local guides. Rates are as follows: lodge rooms are $65/double, studio apartment is $110/double, cabins begin at $300/day; drift boats are $75/day including local shuttle; kickboats are $40/day including local shuttle; river shuttles range from $15 to $30, depending on distance. For guide service it's $350/day.

• WOLF CREEK LODGE, offers the most luxurious lodgings on the Missouri River. It can comfortably sleep four to six people. Rates for 2002 were $500/night and reservations are taken through Missouri River Expeditions or the Missouri Trout Shop and Lodge. If guests prefer not to cook, food can be ordered from the Trout Shop Cafe and delivered for a small fee.

• THE FLY FISHERS' INN, Rick and Lynne Pasquale, proprietors, 2629 Old U.S. Highway 91, Cascade, MT 59421; Tel. 406-468-2529, e-mail: ffi@flyfishersinn.com, website: www.flyfishersinn.com, Packages including guiding, lodging and meals, based on double occupancy per angler were $1,150 for three days of fishing/four nights; $1,450 for four days of fishing/five nights; $1,750 five days of fishing/six nights; and $2,000 for six days of fishing/seven nights. Everything on the menu is made fresh daily, including the bread. Dinners are five courses and interesting wines and beer are available. The kitchen prepares meals so outstanding that some preparations have been featured in *Sunset* magazine.

• PETE CARDINAL, Missouri River Angler, 2675 Craig River Rd., Wolf Creek, MT 59648; Tel. 406-235-9055, was one of the first guides on the Missouri River. He was the person that introduced us to the stream. Pete received his Masters Degree in Fisheries Management from Montana State University and later worked as a biologist on the stream. There are few people with as much knowledge about fishing the Missouri as Pete.

• MISSOURI RIVERSIDE OUTFITTERS & LODGE, Arnie Gidlow, proprietor, 3103 Old U.S. Highway 91, Cascade, MT 59421; Tel. 406-468-9385, and web site: missouririverside.com, e-mail: mobows@mcn.net, has rooms, meals, and guided drift fishing offered individually or as a package. Room rates begin at $75/person. Guided drift fishing for one or two anglers, which includes lunches and beverages, was $335/day. Packaged trips, which included full guide service, lodging and all meals, were $470/single and $520/double for one day; $940/single and $1,040/double for two days.

• MONTANA RIVER OUTFITTERS, Craig Madsen, proprietor, is located at 923 10th Avenue, N. Great Falls, MT 59401. Tel. 406-761-1677, 800-800-8218, FAX 406-452-3833. During the summer, it has a satellite operation at 515 Recreation Road, Wolf Creek, MT 50648; Tel. 406-235-4350, 800-800-4350, e-mail: craigm@montana.com, website: www.montanariver-outfitters.com. At the Wolf Creek location, there is a full fly shop with boat, raft and kickboat rentals, guide service, several RV sites, motel rooms and housekeeping cabins. A day of guided float fishing for two anglers is $360. Motel rooms are $40/night and cabins are $89/night. The boats available to rent are too many to list, with some suitable for large parties interested in river touring. For the flyfisher, there were canoes for $40/day, kick boats for $40/day and drift boats for $75/day. Neale Streeks, the fly-fishing writer, guides for this outfit. Some of our readers have been guided by Neale and reported excellent service. Montana River Outfitters also provides services on other streams including the

South Fork of the Flathead and the Smith rivers.

• HOLTER LAKE LODGE,1350 Beartooth Road, Wolf Creek, MT 59648; Tel. 406-235-4331, has motel rooms and a restaurant. The lodge sits on a hill with a view of Holter Lake. We have not eaten here recently, but understand the food is good. Room rates were $55/single and $67/double. Website: www.osprey-expeditions.com

• GARY FRITZ, OSPREY EXPEDITIONS, PO Box 593, Helena, MT 59624; Tel. 800-315-8502, website: www.osprey-expeditions.com, guides on the Missouri, the Blackfoot and Smith rivers. We fished with him on the Smith and found him to be attentive and capable. Some of our readers have fished with Gary on the Missouri and gave him high marks. His charge for a day of drift fishing was $325. E-mail: ospreyexp@aol.com

• To benefit the Missouri River, contact: The Missouri River Foundation, Box 163 Cascade, MT 59421.

Camping

There are numerous places to camp along the river at developed accesses. The one thing they have in common is that they lack tall trees that provide shade, the exception being the campground below Holter Dam. This campground and the one at Craig are the most popular and securing a site at either one of these during the height of the season can be difficult. Through the years, willows have grown thick at some of the accesses providing partial shade, but anyone camping for an extended period should consider bringing a shade shelter of some kind.

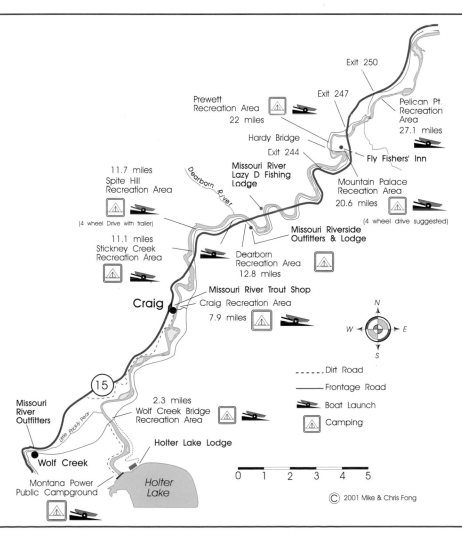

SOUTH FORK BOISE RIVER

SOUTH FORK BOISE RIVER

Nearly all of the major trout streams in the West are tail-water fisheries, meaning the water flowing in the stream comes from an artificial impoundment. If trout populations are strong, the streams are usually heavily fished. Part of the pressure is brought on by professional guides who often provide services that clients couldn't or wouldn't do for themselves. This is often a good arrangement as both parties benefit. There comes a time, however, when it is reasonable to ask, how much is too much? Even if a river is large, is a constant parade of boats a good thing? One stream, which you won't have to worry about professionally-guided anglers, is the South Fork of the Boise River in Idaho near Mountain Home. An ordinance prohibits professional guides from working on the river downstream of Anderson Ranch Dam. From time to time, you see anglers fishing with one another in what appears to be a tutorial situation, but if these "outlaw" guides thought twice, they'd be foolish to jeopardize their livelihood.

The South Fork of the Boise below Anderson Ranch Dam is like many other western rivers in that it is primarily used to transport water for irrigating farmlands. During summer, the water is too high for the stream to be waded safely and fishing is done from boats. For anglers who prefer to wade, autumn and early winter are the best times to fish as flows are reduced. The trout populations cannot be compared favorably with the more famous western tailwater fisheries, but in the lower flows of late season the fish become more concentrated and excellent fishing can be had.

The character of the stream is different depending upon where you choose to fish. There are a few long, deep, slow-moving pools, which are best fished with a small boat or inflatable as it allows you to reach the opposite bank where it seems the rainbows most often rise. For the most

The South Fork of the Boise River flowing from Anderson Ranch Reservoir offers fishing for wild rainbow trout in less crowded conditions compared to western streams of similar quality fishing.

part, the riffles and runs can be effectively fished by wading and having a boat is not a necessity. Besides the fishing, one of the strongest draws of the South Fork of the Boise River below Anderson Ranch Dam is the opportunity to camp next to the water. If you like to set up camp or have a RV, you have the unique opportunity of being lulled to sleep by gurgling water disturbed only by the splash of a feeding trout. It's not a place where anglers sleep deep into the morning. The report on the South Fork of the Boise appeared in Volume III, Number 5, September 1994. Chris and I have fished the river since because of the good fishing it continues to provide.

SOUTH FORK BOISE RIVER

A trout stream which you may not be familiar with is the South Fork of the Boise River flowing from Anderson Ranch Reservoir near Mountain Home in Idaho. There is a local ordinance preventing professional guides and outfitters to work on this stream. This regulation has been in effect for many years and may be the main reason why the South Fork, as it is called by the locals, receives little publicity. Chris and I fished here first in November of 1979 in the company of some members of the Boise Valley Fly Fishers. That outing was one of our most exciting excursions.

From the town of Boise, we drove about forty miles south on Highway 84. At the junction with Highway 20, we turned east toward Sun Valley. It was late in November and patches of snow from a passing storm remained. The air temperature following the storm stayed very cold and where the pavement ended and the descent into the canyon began, we encountered ice. Clayne Baker from Boise was our driver. He engaged the 4-wheel drive and we inched our way down the twisty course. There was barely enough traction to negotiate the worst places. At outer hairpin curves, there was nothing between the road's edge and a drop of hundreds of feet into the canyon. I think everybody was a little nervous. Riding on the passenger seat next to Clayne, the side nearest the mountain, I kept a firm grip on the door handle ready to exit the vehicle at the slightest hint of trouble. I don't know what anyone else was thinking because no one spoke a word.

Once down to the river, you could almost feel the consensus relief in the air. However, the perils of the descent were quickly forgotten as rainbows came readily to our flies. This was mainly fishing over midges, and although there was some surface feeding, most of the trout were caught by nymphing. In the afternoon, the weather began to deteriorate. First came wind and then sleet. We knew it would soon turn to snow. There was little time to waste. We got out of our waders, quickly packed our things and started the drive out of the canyon.

The ice was now being lubricated and the ascent made the trip down seem like a piece of cake. At one of the hairpin curves, a sedan was nestled against the hill unable to continue. These people were being helped by anglers in a 4-wheel-drive jeep. A tow rope was connected to the car and they were making progress. Clayne stopped to see if more help was needed. As we stepped out, the ice-coated road was so slippery it was impossible to stand without sliding down the sloping road. Our help was not needed and we resumed our slow and precarious drive out. When we got to the top, someone discovered a bottle of rum beneath the back seat. Since I wasn't driving, I took a shot. Ordinarily I don't drink rum, but this was an exception.

Fishing during a snowfall.

That trip didn't hinder us from returning to the South Fork of the Boise, but it wasn't until early October 1994 that we made another visit. This time we camped in our van conversion for a few days because the South Fork is so well suited for this. From the dam downstream, a dirt road follows the stream for about 12 miles before it leaves the river. Along this main dirt road are many spurs that take you to the river's edge.

Chris with a rainbow she is about to release.

There are shade trees at most places but no drinking water anywhere in the canyon. All the areas for camping are completely unimproved with the exception of the Village Float Boat Access, where there are outhouses.

The South Fork of the Boise River is a large tailwater trout fishery. Its autumn make-up is like a classic freestone stream. Beside riffles entering runs and moderately deep pools, there are some pools deep enough where the current is noticeably slowed. From the dam downstream for a mile and a half, there were thick beds of aquatic weeds. Downstream of this, these wavy grasses, often seen in spring creeks, were almost absent. I point this out because there may be different aquatic animals in the first mile and a half of stream than farther downstream. In the reduced autumn flows, the South Fork of the Boise can be waded across at the tail of most pools and at wide places. The bottom is composed of bedrock, cobble, and gravel. Felt-soled waders give adequate traction, but studded soles improve footing. During the high flow of summer, wading is difficult. Good fishing is possible for those who drift.

Chris and I arrived to the South Fork at 5:30 on Sunday evening, October 10. It was warm and without any wind. With an hour of light left to fish, we drove to a spot about a mile below the Village Float Boat Access. Here a riffle entered a pool with the deepest water near the road. While Chris watched with her camera, I waded out to the head of the riffle. There were no fish rising so I tied on a #12 soft hackle with a green body and brown hackle. Fishing a traditional wet fly swing, I hooked and landed two rainbows measuring 14 inches in a half hour. As darkness began to set in, a few fish started rising. The fish in the riffle seemed small, but I saw what appeared to be a much larger fish on the edge of the riffle near the bank where the water dropped into the pool. In order to get the soft hackle to drift slowly into this lie, I waded back toward the bank to set up my swing. Had I stayed in water faster than the fish were holding in and made my presentation, the fly would swim too fast past the fish to encourage a strike. On the second cast, I had a tug and pulled back too hard leaving the fly in the fish's mouth.

That evening, we camped at the Village Float Boat Access. There was a large RV already parked, occupied by two anglers from Riverside, California. They had been on the South Fork a year earlier and experienced good fishing. The largest rainbow that they landed the year before was 24 inches. They said the fishing this year was much slower for them. After darkness fell, the wind began to blow, and it blew through the night with strong gusts.

The wind was still blowing when we awoke at 7:00 and it threatened to rain. After breakfast, we drove into Mountain Home to have a noisy U-Joint replaced. We arrived back to the stream at 12:30 and fished the long, slow pool across from the Village. The Village, as it is referred to, is the area where people were housed who built the dam. At the end of this pool, there is a turnout where a couple of vehicles can be parked.

By now the wind had died. There was a sparse hatch of PMDs, a smaller, light colored mayfly and some Baetis. The water temperature was 49 degrees. A few fish rose consistently, but most did so irregularly. The fish that fed most often on the surface were along the far bank. I waded knee deep water to cross at the tail of the pool and then took a position slightly upstream of the nearest riser. By casting across and making an aerial, upstream reach, I adjusted for the slower flow along the bank where the fish fed. An 18-inch rainbow took my #20 Green Sparkle Dun after several casts. It put up a good, strong fight before it was released.

Farther upstream other fish rose along the far bank, but they were difficult to approach. The pool deepened quickly and the only presentation that could be made was a quartering upstream cast. These trout were extremely wary and would not tolerate this angle of presentation. They acted like selective trout found in spring creeks. One upstream cast and they would not rise again. I made an attempt to approach these trout from the bank, but limbs from overhanging trees made

Our first visit to the South Fork of the Boise was in the company of members of the Boise Valley Flyfishers including Janet and Marty.

After several days of fishing, we realized that many of the larger rainbows hooked came from water beneath the overhang of tree limbs.

casting impossible. The only way to get a downstream angle to these fish was to use a boat. A belly boat might have worked, but a personal inflatable that is designed to be used with oars would have been better. We did not bring such a craft with us on this trip. This pool was not the only one hosting larger than average size trout that were difficult to reach. There were other slow, deep pools where good fish also rose on the far bank. If you have a suitable inflatable and enjoy fishing for some very challenging trout, these rainbows are worth a try.

The hatch petered out at 2:00. Using a #12 green bodied caddis emerger, I landed two smaller rainbows with a traditional wet fly swing. These trout were taken from the side of the river nearest the road, which was more open and easier to fish. Along the edge of the pool were many large odd-shaped boulders making footing difficult. A wading staff would have come in handy. The water temperature was 49 degrees, the same as the day before.

At 4:30, we drove along the stream looking for a place to fish during the evening. After looking at several options, I choose some water about a mile farther downstream from where we fished the previous night. At the end of a spur, we parked right alongside the stream on a bank overlooking the water. A riffle entered around an island flowing through a flat pool. I couldn't see any hatch activity and rises were infrequent. A few small, brown caddis were on the water so I tied on a #14 brown caddis emerger. In three quarters of an hour, I landed three small rainbows with the largest about 13 inches. We spent the night again at the Village Float Boat Access. While Chris cooked dinner, it began to sprinkle. The daytime air temperature reached a high in the mid 60s. That night it got down to the mid 40s.

The clouds during the night gave way to a clear morning. We awoke at 9:00. After breakfast, we drove downstream near to where we fished the night before. A group of men had set up camp at the end of a pool and some were fishing. They had not caught a trout, but had hooked some white fish. They must have gotten up early to fish because upon our arrival, they retired for breakfast. Around their tents, I noticed some belly boats. Later, we saw a couple of them drifting. In the stretch they drifted, there were none of the long, deep pools where trout can often be found rising.

Crossing easily at the tail of the pool, we headed upstream. At an island there was a run on the inside that was deep enough to hold fish, but casts with a dry and then with a nymph didn't bring a strike. At the tail of the next pool, fish were rising regularly, but they were whitefish. The rise forms were quick and splashy. At the head of this pool was another island with an even better run on the inside. Where the water of the side run met the main current, we saw a couple of fish working on top. We could not entice them with a dry fly, but I hooked and landed a 16-inch rainbow on a #10 Martinez nymph fished with a split shot 12 inches above the fly. The fish took the fly as it was swinging.

Right after I landed this fish, a Department of Fish & Game boat came down along the opposite bank. A fish shocking program was being conducted. As we watched, they recovered two good size rainbows in a 50-yard stretch. Shortly after this, a Boise angler whom we met years ago came by. He was working his way downstream with a Muddler Minnow. The fishing was slow for him, but he said he was using the large fly hoping to attract a big rainbow. He said rainbows as large as ten pounds are known to reside in the river. After visiting for while, he continued downstream.

We fished the riffle entering the pool and hooked a few whitefish and then headed downstream ourselves. At the inside run we passed earlier, the angler fishing the Muddler had switched to a dry. He said he landed two rainbows with the largest measuring 14 inches. After a farewell, he headed back from where he came and we fished the main stem riffle on the other side of this island. Still using the Martinez nymph, we landed six whitefish, but no trout. We returned to the north bank where we waded across earlier and then walked back to the van. Along the way, we could see some casualties from the shocking. Three dead trout, all of them larger than 14 inches, lay along the shallows.

This part of the river features many long, open pools and the cobble bottom is covered with fine moss. It is more difficult to wade than the water upstream. For us, the fishing upstream was more productive. At the time of our visit, the river was running at 600 cfs, typical for a year when there was good storage in the reservoir. In drought years, after releases from the dam are reduced in early September, flows of 300 cfs are common. This makes wading much easier and concentrates the trout in the runs and pools. Contact the fly-shops in Boise to find the current river conditions.

After lunch, we rested, planning to be on the water at 4:00. We drove back to the run we fished the first evening where I broke off a good fish. Using a #14 Bird's Nest, I hooked three good rainbows with the largest a hooked-jaw male around 20 inches. I fished the Bird's Nest with a short-line nymphing method. Two white fish were also landed. As shadows fell on the water, a few fish began to rise. I switched to a #14 Nelson Caddis and landed three more rainbows, the largest about 15 inches. That night, we drove to Mountain Home to stay in a motel and clean up.

After sleeping in a bit, we went back to the South Fork at 11:00. Clouds began to build and we took the opportunity to photograph scenics along the river. While Chris took photos, I probed with a nymph and caught a few whitefish. We explored areas both upstream and downstream of Village with very little to show for our efforts. There were no fish rising anywhere we looked.

At 4:30 we went back to the Village Float Boat Access. Right across from the access was promising water being fished by two anglers. It was not too difficult to wade to the opposite side to the best runs, but these anglers fished only to the middle of the river. Chris and I went downstream to a riffle that they already fished.

Using a #16 Green Sparkle Dun, Chris landed a 14-inch rainbow and two whitefish in the first half hour. The run of good water upstream on the opposite bank continued down to where we fished. We decided it would be worth the effort to wade across. The water was deeper and swifter in midstream than upstream, so we locked our arms for support and made our way across. In the falling light, fish rose. These secondary runs that are still connected to the main flow are the kinds of places where we consistently caught our largest fish. Still using the Sparkle Dun, Chris hooked and landed a 19-inch rainbow after a long fight. Just upstream at the next break in the current, I landed a rainbow and a cutthroat. They also took a Sparkle dun and each was about 13 inches. We could see a few more fish rising upstream, but it was getting dark. To have enough light to wade back across safely, we left these fish still feeding.

That night it got down to 40 degrees and it rained lightly. During breakfast, the Fish & Game shocking crew launched their boat and made ready for another sampling. I asked them not to start right across the river because I wanted to fish this water. They were kind enough to oblige, and this put me at ease. On their sampling earlier in the week, they recovered about 125 rainbows and a ton of whitefish in a five-mile drift. Most of the larger rainbows they shocked came from relatively shallow water where there were branches from trees shading the water. As we waded across to the water we hadn't fished the night before, their noisy generator started and their boat shoved off.

Unlike the night before, fish were not rising so we fished the seams and pockets that seemed likely to hold fish. I chose a #14 Bird's Nest and placed an indicator five feet above the fly. A small shot was pinched about a foot above the Bird's Nest. On the second or third cast, I had a grab and a large rainbow shot 25 yards downstream and made a water-clearing leap right next to the Fish & Game boat. It looked well over 20 inches. The rainbow had so much line out on me so fast

that I didn't have a chance. As I gave chase, it broke me off around a rock.

As I was retying my leader, Chris hooked and landed a 17-inch rainbow. After the customary photos and release, I hooked and landed a 19 incher. Her fish, like mine, held in a shallow run near the bank where branches made it difficult to place a fly. After some thought, we concluded that almost every decent fish we caught came from similar water. The exception was the rainbow that came from the long, deep pool opposite the Village.

Driving down into the canyon to reach the South Fork of the Boise can be treacherous after snow starts to fall and the road ices up.

SUMMARY

The span of four days is not long enough to make a conclusive evaluation about the fishing in any stream. This is the reason we suggest that anglers who anticipate fishing any stream call a local fly shop to inquire about present conditions before making a lengthy trip. Like all our western streams, the South Fork has had to endure both high and low water years during the 90s. Our visit took place between the seasons. Days were still warm and the night temperatures had not yet fallen below freezing. This is normally not a time when fishing is at its autumn prime. It is only when freezing temperatures are reached that fall hatches become sustained and trout seem to be stimulated to feed heavily. For that reason, I would advise you to inquire on the temperature extremes from a fly shop in Boise before determining if the chance for prime fishing exists. These temperatures are also listed in most newspapers.

If you are equipped to camp in cool weather or have an RV, the South Fork of the Boise can provide a fishing/camping trip with little competition from other anglers except locals who fish mainly on weekends. From Anderson Dam downstream, the South Fork of the Boise is under special regulations. Only single, barbless hook lures or flies can be used. The limit is two trout, but none may measure from 12 to 20 inches. At the season closing at the end of November, the stream remains open to catching whitefish. If you catch a trout during the whitefish season, you must release it. Scheduled flights serve Boise where rental cars are available. Morris Air (800/466-7747) often has very attractive prices. It flies from most major cities in the West.

Accommodations

The motels in Mountain Home are mostly old. Newer facilities are found at the junction of Highway 20 with Highway 84.
• SLEEP INN, 1180 US 20, Mountain Home 83647; Tel. 208-587-9743, 800-221-2222, had rooms beginning around $50/night.
• THE BEST WESTERN FOOTHILL MOTOR INN, 1080 US Highway 20, Mountain Home, ID, 83647; Tel.

208-587-5774, FAX 208-587-8477, rates began at around $55/night. The rooms are smaller at Sleep Inn, but each room has a refrigerator. The downstairs room refrigerators are filled with drinks and guests are charged for whatever is used. Discounted rates are available at both motels. There is a restaurant next to the Best Western.

Fly Shops

There are a number of fly shops in Boise that can provide fishing information on the South Fork of the Boise River. These include:
• ANGLERS, 7097 Overland Road, Boise, ID 83709 Tel. 208-323-6768), web-site: www.anglersline.net,

• BEAR CREEK FLY SHOP, Boise, ID 83703; Tel. 208-853-8704,
• IDAHO ANGLER, 16825 Vista Ave., Boise, ID 83705 Tel. 208-389-9957, 800-787-9957, website: www.idahoangler.com.

Mike gets ready to net a rainbow that was hooked far upstream with a nymph fished below an indicator.

In the autumn when flows are reduced, there are some long, slow-moving pools where fish rise regularly and can be tempted with a dry fly.

The rainbows of the South Fork are fit fish.

The trees along the river begin to get their autumn colors in early October.

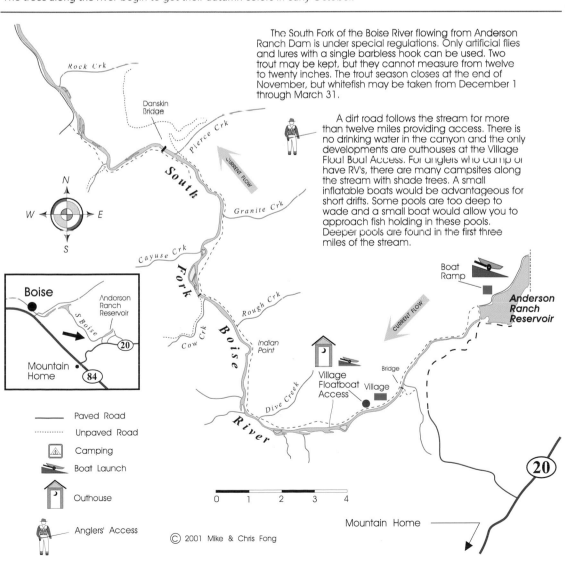

The South Fork of the Boise River flowing from Anderson Ranch Dam is under special regulations. Only artificial flies and lures with a single barbless hook can be used. Two trout may be kept, but they cannot measure from twelve to twenty inches. The trout season closes at the end of November, but whitefish may be taken from December 1 through March 31.

A dirt road follows the stream for more than twelve miles providing access. There is no drinking water in the canyon and the only developments are outhouses at the Village Float Boat Access. For anglers who camp or have RV's, there are many campsites along the stream with shade trees. A small inflatable boats would be advantageous for short drifts. Some pools are too deep to wade and a small boat would allow you to approach fish holding in these pools. Deeper pools are found in the first three miles of the stream.

Boise

Anderson Ranch Reservoir

S Boise

20

Mountain Home

84

——— Paved Road

········· Unpaved Road

⚠ Camping

⛵ Boat Launch

☾ Outhouse

🎣 Anglers' Access

0 1 2 3 4

© 2001 Mike & Chris Fong

Mountain Home

UPPER ROGUE RIVER

10 *South Central Oregon*

UPPER ROGUE RIVER

*I*n the early 1990s and continuing for most of the decade, the Rogue River in southern Oregon produced some of the best steelhead fishing on the West Coast. By the end of November 1994, more than 10,000 steelhead had passed beyond Gold Ray Dam near Medford. From Gold Ray Dam, it is approximately thirty miles to Lost Creek Dam and the Cole Rivers Fish Hatchery, the upstream limit of steelhead migration. But these numbers of steelhead do not tell the whole story. Only 25% of the steelhead returning to this stretch of river are hatchery reared. Because the hatchery required only 300 adult steelhead to perpetuate the hatchery runs, large numbers of returning steelhead were trucked downstream to Gold Ray Dam so anglers would have another chance at catching them. The returns were so abundant, steelhead were transported not once, but twice. Fish were released on Thursdays for the benefit of weekend anglers. It would have been very difficult to find steelhead fishing equal to that which took place on the Rogue in the autumn of 1994.

During September and October, fishing on the Rogue from Gold Ray Dam to Cole Rivers Hatchery is restricted to the use of barbless hook, artificial flies. Anglers can use any type of rod and reel, but are not allowed to use metal-core lines, any added weights or attachments except a bubble or similar floating device. Two steelhead may be kept, but they must be fin-clipped. All wild steelhead must be released unharmed. Any rainbow trout sixteen inches or larger is considered a steelhead.

The average size of a steelhead returning to the upper Rogue River measures between eighteen and twenty-two inches. Many anglers familiar with steelhead say these fish are some of the hardest fighting for their size anywhere. Because the fish are not large, 5- to 7- weight systems are often used. The techniques that are effective

A sweep of this pool with a fast-sinking shooting taper and a heavily-weighted nymph drew a strike from a steelhead.

Not that many years ago, it was against regulations to fish from a boat on the Rogue River above Gold Ray Dam. This regulation was changed allowing fishing from a boat, making drifting, by far, the best way to fish the river.

depend on prevailing weather conditions and the controlled releases of water from the dam.

We arrived at Shady Cove on Saturday evening, October 16. Traveling in our van conversion, we stayed at the Fly Casters RV Park. That night the temperature dropped into the mid 40s. The next morning, after having breakfast at Mac's, a diner in Shady Cove, we drove upstream. Crossing over the Highway 62 Bridge that spans the river below the hatchery, we turned onto the dirt road that led upstream. There were a couple of spin-fishers working a pool, and across the river we saw a flyfisher. He was using a sink-tip line, but was too far away for us to see his fly. As he walked downstream to work another run, he carried a small steelhead at his side. The site of the fish was a promising sign. As we walked back to the vehicle to find some water to fish, Chris noticed one of our rear tires was slowly deflating. Before it went flat, I got the jack underneath and replaced the tire with the spare. The nearest place to get the tire fixed was in Medford and that is where we headed.

It was about 1:00 when we returned to the river. First we stopped at the Rogue Elk Park, where camping is allowed, to take a few photos. We noted that coin-operated showers were present. Then we had lunch at the day-use area downstream from the Highway 62 bridge. The day had warmed into the mid 60s and we watched two trout fishers land a number of rainbows on dries over a Baetis hatch. After eating, we planned to go upstream to the runs below the hatchery where we went in the morning only to find that another one of our tires was losing air. Again, we drove back to Medford. By the time we got back to the river, there was only time to fish for less than an hour. We tried the run immediately below the Highway 62 Bridge without a strike. That night we stayed at the Rogue River RV Park.

On Monday morning, we awoke at 7:45. Without eating breakfast, we drove to McGregor Park, a day-use area on the west side of the river downstream of the hatchery. Parking in one of the paved lots, we made a five-minute walk to one of the runs upstream. There were no other anglers in sight. I chose a #7 outfit matched to a high-density shooting taper. At the end of the 3x tippet, I tied on a #4 Black Rubberleg. The stream at this point was fifty feet across. I started fishing at the head of a riffle using a short-line nymphing method. Sometimes steelhead hold in riffles, but I could not entice a fish from the broken water. In order to cover more water with each cast, I lengthened the line so that the thirty-foot shooting taper and ten feet of running line lay outside

the tip top. Making casts across the current followed by an upstream mend, the heavily weighted Rubberleg gained depth and then swung slowly across the flow. I began to work my way down the run. On the fourth cast, as the fly drifted into a slick next to some runny water, a steelhead struck. I was surprised the steelhead didn't fight harder than it did. It was a female fish of nineteen inches. From the time the fish struck to the time when it was subdued lasted only a few minutes.

I worked down the run another forty feet without a strike. At this point the water got too shallow to hold fish. The river turned away from me toward a steep bank dropping into a corner pool. Gathering all of its volume from many braids, the current ran deep before opening into a large pool. Positioning myself at the head of the pool, I began to make ninety-foot casts across the current. After each succeeding cast and swing of the fly, I would take a few steps downstream and make another sweep of the pool. Near the tail of the pool, a steelhead took the fly as it drifted slowly across the flow. This was also a female steelhead several inches longer than the one I hooked earlier. It fought well and cleared the water a couple of times during the fight. By now the sun that was shielded from the water by a high bank began to light up the pool. The water temperature was 46 degrees. We returned to the vehicle to have breakfast.

After eating, we went to the hatchery. Tim Wright, a fisheries biologist, told us that 2,300 summer-run steelhead had returned to the hatchery. In a few days, 2,000 of these fish were going to be trucked downstream to Gold Ray Dam to be released so anglers could have another shot at them. Tim was very helpful in answering our questions about the runs of steelhead on the Rogue.

At noon, we headed for Eugene. Our appetite for steelhead fishing was stimulated and we would have stayed on the Rogue to fish, but we had a date to address the McKenzie Fly Fishers in Eugene that evening. Chris and I enjoyed meeting the members of the club and renewing acquaintances with fellow anglers. The next morning, we went to The Caddis Fly Angling Shop to see if they had any recommendations on where to fish locally. Opportunities were not great, so we decided to visit the Cushner Museum in Florence on the coast. The museum was opened by appointment only by calling (541/997-6349), which the fly shop did for us. The Cushner Collection is comprised of flyfishing equipment, angling artwork, photographs and flies created by important anglers from this country and abroad. In the hands of others, these items would not be significant. But during his life, William Cushner tastefully framed much of his collection, placing together artwork and flies into pleasing compositions of historical importance. After his death in 1992, the operation of the museum fell into the hands of his son-in-law, Jack Smrekar. Without funding to maintain the museum, Jack was in the process of finding the collection a permanent home with regular hours. If you are in the area, a visit is well worth your time. Jack does custom framing of museum quality should you need his services. That evening, we drove back to Eugene and headed upstream along the McKenzie River. We spent the night at a RV park about fifteen miles out of town.

We slept late the next morning and then made further inquiries about the local fishing. There were no alternatives to match the steelhead fishing on the Rogue, so we drove back to Shady Cove, arriving around 3:00. To line up a guide for Friday, we went to the Fishing Hole and met Jack Jermain, the owner. He arranged for us to fish with a guide from Ashland. For that afternoon, Jack suggested we fish the river across from the

In addition to steelhead and salmon, the Rogue also has resident rainbow trout and sea-run cutthroat. Here Al Perryman plays a cutthroat

Elk Rogue Cafe. This run was immediately downstream from the Rogue Elk Campground.

The shadows of evening were falling on the pool when we arrived. There was not a breath of wind and the air temperature was in the low 60s. It was as pleasant an evening as you will find on the Rogue in October. We saw no fish roll as they often do in low light so I chose to fish a Black Rubber Leg with a high-density shooting taper again. Two steelhead measuring a little more than twenty inches were landed. Both fish were holding on the far side of a tailout just before the water funneled into a riffle. In order to get a good drift to these fish, it was necessary to make an aerial, upstream reach after the cast and before the line settled to the water to set up the drift. Both fish took the fly just as it was beginning to swing. We had no other strikes that evening. The night was spent again at the Rogue River RV Park.

After breakfast the next morning, I tied flies to replace those that were lost. At 10:00, Jack Jermain came by and introduced us to David Roberts and C. J. Smolen, local flyfishers who were very familiar with this stretch of the Rogue. David ties flies for the Fishing Hole when he isn't working as a mechanic and was recently featured in a local newspaper article about steelhead fishing on the Rogue. One of David's creations called an Ugly Bug was mentioned in the article as being very effective. It is essentially a modified Rubberleg tied on a #8 hook. This fly can be fished a number of ways, but one of the most productive techniques is with an indicator. The method is no different from fishing a heavily-weighted nymph upstream for trout. David tied a few Ugly Bugs for us and offered to take us for a drift on Sunday. Unfortunately, we were not able to accept his offer because of other commitments. C. J. Smolen is a custom carpet installer and offered to fish with us that afternoon.

Mike releases a female steelhead caught on an Ugly Bug, a fly similar to a Black Rubber Leg.

There wasn't a cloud in the sky when we began fishing at 2:00. At the first place we tried downstream of the hatchery, we didn't touch a fish. C. J. used a floating line to fish a heavy stonefly nymph with a #8 Glo Bug on an eighteen-inch dropper. The dropper was tied to the bend of the hook of the nymph. At the next run downstream, we hooked and landed several rainbows to twelve inches and three steelhead to twenty-six and a half inches. With a girth of thirteen and three quarters of an inch, this male steelhead weighed about six pounds according to the Polly Rosborough "Get-It Right Weight Chart." These handy charts are available at fly shops and I keep mine in the same zip lock packet that displays my fishing license.

To end the day, we went to a run downstream of the Elk Rogue Park. C. J. landed a steelhead about eighteen inches long and Chris played a fish right to the bank before it got loose. The steelhead took a large Rubberleg and looked to be in the twenty-four- to twenty-five-inch range. The water temperature was 45 degrees.

We drove back to Shady Cove and had dinner at the Two Pine Restaurant. This restaurant had just opened in August and featured pork and beef ribs, chicken and steak. A complete dinner with a half order of ribs was $7.95. This included a medium size drink plus ice cream for dessert. We found the ribs a bit dry, but everything else, including the service, was good. If you seek more formal dining, the Bel Di's Restaurant is in the middle of town. The menu is more varied and they have a wine list.

On Friday morning, we did our laundry at the Rogue River RV Park where we spent the night. At 1:00, we met Jonah Hague of Noah's World of Water. His drift boat was on a trailer behind his Suburban. On our afternoon drift with Noah beginning at 2:00 at Dodge Bridge on Agate Road, we caught two steelhead and a few trout. One of the native rainbows measured twenty-inches. We fished Rubberlegs and Ugly Bugs. Infrequently, large sea-run cutthroat are also taken on the upper Rogue.

There was one rapid on our drift called Rattlesnake that discourages inexperienced boaters from making this run. If you drift on your own and have limited experience, there are other sections of the river that are less threatening. A popular drift is from Shady Cove, where there is a public launch, to Dodge Bridge. The main reason we hired Noah was to find a reliable guide should our readers want to drift. We found Noah to be a competent boatman and I liked the way he helped Chris when we stopped to fish by wading. Flies and lunch are provided and the fee is $125/angler, two to a boat. Noah has a couple of guides specializing in flyfishing and you should state this preference if you book with him. Mark Swisher is Noah's top flyfishing guide. Mark's most successful clients last year landed highs of

An angler fishes in the last light of a warm autumn evening.

twelve to fourteen steelhead in one day's fishing. Those days were in late September and in early October.

Another guide we recommend is Al Perryman of Perryman's Guide Service. We have fished with Al for many years in California, where he was born and fished extensively, and in Oregon, where he now resides. We made a short drift with Al the day after fishing with Noah and hooked a jack salmon and steelhead. His best day with flyfishing clients last year was more than ten steelhead and that was a day in early October. September and October are the most desirable months to fish the upper Rogue and good guides are in high demand. During this period, reservations well in advance of a trip are recommended.

Fishing from a boat, whether your own or with a guide, is advantageous. For years, fishing from a boat on the upper Rogue was against regulations. Current rules allow anglers to fish from a boat and this has made the fishing much more productive for fly fishers. To reach some of the better lies requires deep wading and long casts. With a boat, difficult wading can be eliminated and casts can be shorter. This has made the upper Rogue a stream that can produce for flyfishers of all skill levels.

As with all steelhead fishing, there are times on any stream that might prove to be more productive. The Inside Angler does its best to point out advantageous times and also to explain factors that might influence the fishing. On the upper Rogue, productive fishing usually begins in mid August with the arrival of good numbers of steelhead and can last through mid November. Good fishing can be experienced earlier downstream. For anglers fishing on foot, releases are normally reduced in late September making wading and access to runs much easier. These conditions can bring about some of the fastest fishing of the season as water temperatures are in the mid 50s making the fish aggressive and full of fight.

Each year in early October, the water temperature is reduced at Lost Creek Dam to 43 degrees to stimulate salmon to spawn. Normally, this takes place in the second week of the month. This lowering of the water temperature coincides with the heaviest runs of steelhead in the upper river. In water temperatures measuring above 50 degrees, steelhead can be lured to the surface to take a fly and they are normally robust. Anglers preferring to fish dry flies for steelhead should take particular note of this. When the water temperature becomes lower than fifty degrees and begins to approach forty, the willingness of steelhead to come to the fly is greatly reduced. To deal with this cold water, there are ways to improve your chances. In presenting your fly, try to fish slower and work the holding water more thoroughly. Experienced anglers start with short casts and increase the distance until all the water is covered from that position. Then they take a few steps downstream and repeat the series again. By doing this more precise probing, you stand a better chance of drifting your fly through a fish-holding lie. Another thing you can do is concentrate your fishing in the warmest part of the day. I would even go so far as to suggest that when fishing with a guide, you request the latest start possible so you can fish through the afternoon and early evening. What some anglers do to contend with the low water temperature is fish further downstream. Even with the temperature of the water reduced to 43 degrees at the dam, it would not be unusual to find a four- to six-degree increase to downstream temperatures providing the weather is mild. Good steelhead fishing continues in October below Gold Ray Dam where many steelhead are still migrating upstream.

In September and October 1994, the weather was extremely mild on the upper Rogue. It was still very warm in late September and it never got below freezing in October. In some years, freezing air temperatures can occur by early October with rain a likely possibility. Be sure to call ahead as near to the time of your visit as possible to ask about the weather. Ashland, the home of the award-winning Oregon Shakespeare Festival, is about a 45-minute drive from Shady Cove. The season for the Shakespeare Festival runs through October. For more information on the festival and other seasonal events in Ashland, contact the Ashland Chamber of Commerce, Visitors & Convention Bureau, PO Box 1360, 110 East Main Street, Ashland, OR 97520 (541/482-3486). United Express Airlines (800/241-6522), flies from most major western cities and Horizon Airlines, a subsidiary of Alaska Airlines (800/426-0333), flies from Portland and Seattle to the Jackson County Airport in Medford where rental cars are available.

This darker male fish had been in the river for some time before it was hooked and released in October.

Mike barrels a steelhead.

To receive the best rates, be sure to ask for business, automobile service membership and bank card discounts which can influence prices. In Volume III, Number 6, November 15, 1994, The Inside Angler filed a report on the Holy Water, a trout fishery restricted to flyfishing below Lost Creek Dam. This report may contain information of interest for those contemplating a trip to this area. The trout fishing in the Holy Water can be excellent in the autumn. Good nymph fishing for winter steelhead takes place on the upper Rogue in March and April.

Businesses

• FISHING HOLE, PO Box 1314, Shady Cove, OR 97539; Tel. 541-878-4000 sells fishing equipment and carries a selection of locally tied flies. Good information about flyfishing is provided here. Jack Jermain, owner provides year-around professionally guided fishing trips. Website: www.upperrogue.org

• NOAH'S WORLD OF WATER, PO Box 11, 53 North Main Street, Ashland, OR 97520; Tel. 800-858-2811, offers whitewater trips on nearby rivers. They also offer guide trips for anglers. If you seek their

Restaurants

z• TWO PINES SMOKEHOUSE, 21331 Hwy 62, Shady Cove, OR; Tel. 541-878-7463. Serves good barbequed food.

• BEL DI'S RESTAURANT, 21900 HWY 62, Shady Cove, OR Tel. 541-878-2010 is in the middle of town. The menu is more varied and they have a wine list.

services, be sure to tell them you are a flyfisher. One of their guides specializes in flyfishing. Website: www.noahsrafting.com

• AL PERRYMAN, PERRYMAN'S GUIDE SERVICE, Box 1076, Rogue River, OR 97537; Tel. 541-582-0906, provides guiding primarily for flyfishers. Besides guiding clients personally, Al has guides experienced with taking flyfishers down the river. His rate is $250/two anglers and lunch is not included. Al does provide tackle, leaders and flies.

Lodging

The following are some motels near the upper Rogue River and their approximate rates:

• ROYAL COACHMAN MOTEL, 21906 Highway 62, Shady Cove, OR 97539; Tel. 541-878-2481 has rates beginning at around $45 and some rooms have a kitchenette.

• OBSTINATE J RANCH, 30000 Highway 62, Trail, OR 97541; Tel. 541-878-2718, offers riverside housekeeping cabins starting at about $75/night/two people.

• HOLIDAY INN, 1501 S. Pacific Highway, Medford, OR 97504; Tel. 541-732-1400, has rooms starting at around $50/night.

• ROGUE REGENCY, 2345 Crater Lake Highway, Medford, OR 97504; Tel. 800-535-5805, offers singles beginning at around $65/night and doubles at $75/night.

• MOTEL 6, 2400 Biddle Road, Medford, OR 97504 Tel. 541-779-0550, has rooms for singles at $35/night and doubles are $45/night.

RV Parks

• FLY CASTERS RV PARK, 21655 Crater Lake Highway 62, Shady Cove, OR 97539; Tel. 541-878-2749. Rates were around $18/night with full hookups, including cable TV. Sites along the river were $24/night. We found the facilities well maintained with clean, heated restrooms.

• ROGUE RIVER RV PARK, 21800 Crater Lake Highway 62, Shady Cove, OR 97539. Tel. 800-775-0367. The rate was around $14/night and the grounds and facilities were immaculate.

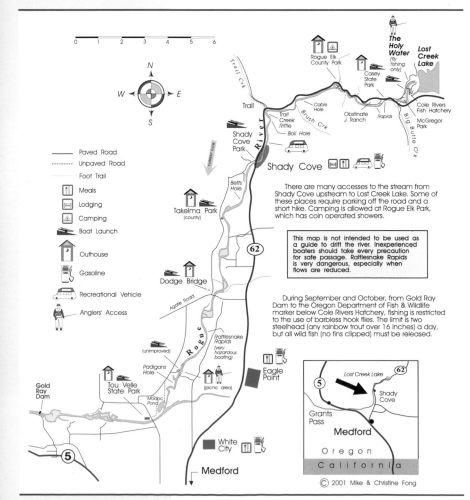